THE BOOK OF
Dragons
& OTHER
Mythical Beasts

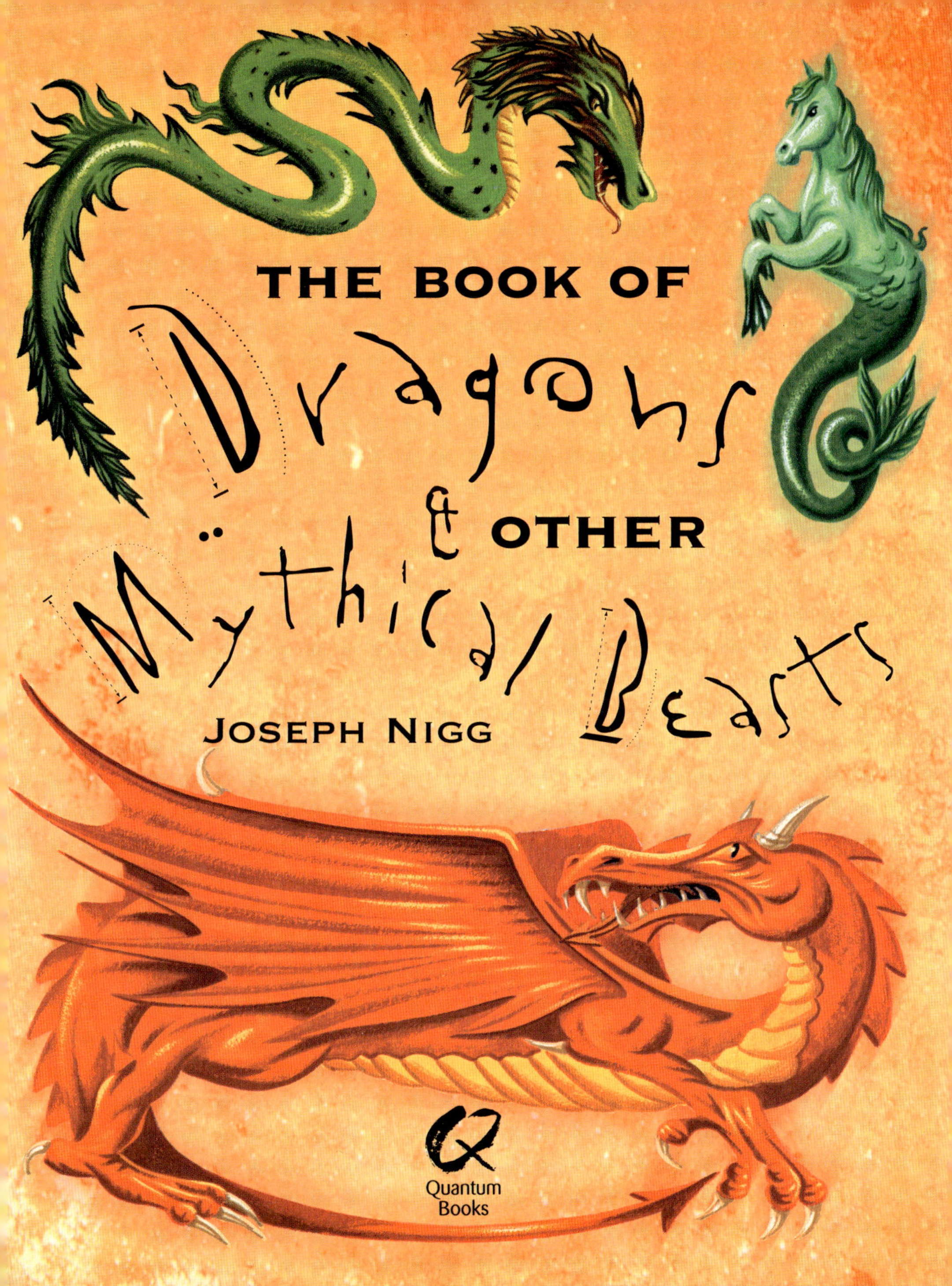
THE BOOK OF
Dragons
& OTHER
Mythical Beasts
JOSEPH NIGG
Quantum
Books

A QUANTUM BOOK

This book is produced by
Quantum Publishing Ltd.
6 Blundell Street
London N7 9BH

This edition printed 2006

ISBN 10: 1-84573-179-4
ISBN 13: 978-1-84573-179-3

QUMBDR

Printed in Singapore
by Star Standard Industries

Contents

Introduction

This book, like the medieval bestiaries, is a book of beasts. Bestiaries, though, were natural histories presenting what were considered at the time to be members of the animal kingdom. They included a number of animals we now regard as mythical. *The Book of Dragons and Other Mythical Beasts*, on the other hand, contains only creatures whose shapes or qualities never existed outside our own imagination.

Dragons, Unicorns, Griffins, the Phoenix, Mermaids, and other ancient beasts continue to fascinate us with their mysterious powers. Called "mythical," "fabulous," "fantastic," and "imaginary," they are like images from dreams—or nightmares.

But why are we so enthralled by creatures of our own making when they cannot even begin to match the abundance and variety of the animal kingdom? Well, for one thing, they are ours. We created them. They are expressions of human fears and of our wonder at the awesome forces of nature. Bestowed with magical qualities, they embody our longings for health, riches, wisdom, and immortality. They are, for us, necessary animals.

Such creatures are all around us in words and images. The eagle-lion Griffin and the fiery Phoenix abound in business names and logos. Figures of the Far Eastern Dragon enhance the décor of Chinese restaurants. These beasts and others of their kind enliven children's literature, fantasy fiction, film, and video games, and are featured on scores of websites. And they are joined by a plethora of newly created fantastic animals known worldwide through films and books. It is a good time for mythical beasts.

Mythological Beginnings

The first generation of imaginary creatures emerged from the world's mythologies. These creatures embodied the powers of the Underworld, the earth, sea, and sky, and personified forces both demonic and divine. Some were involved in Creation itself. The Egyptian Benu rose from the primal waters as a manifestation of the god Atum and became identified with the eternal sun. The Babylonian Dragoness, Tiamat, was the saltwater of the ocean of Chaos. She was mother of a brood of Dragons, demons, scorpion-men, and other monsters. The

hero Marduk slew her, cut her in half, and from her body formed earth and the firmament. The Greek serpent-woman Echidna, too, gave birth to monstrous beings, including the multiheaded Hydra of Lerna, the Chimera, and the Sphinx. These and a host of other monsters populate Greek and Roman mythology.

Prominent in all bodies of mythology is the oldest and most universal of all mythological monsters: The Dragon. Its multiple reptilian forms include creatures that control fertilizing rain—or cause devastating floods: The Nagas of India, the Dragons of China and Japan, and the Rainbow Serpent. While the Dragon of the Far East is generally a beneficent beast, embodying the powers of nature, the Western Dragon commonly represents evil that must be overcome by gods and heroes. The beast spread beyond myth and into folklore and legend, as in the tales of Siegfried, Beowulf, and Saints George, Martha, and Margaret.

Hearsay Animals

As ancient Greek myths gradually diminished in power, another generation of imaginary animals was being born; these evolved in Western literature and art over millennia.

Travelers returning from Egypt, Ethiopia, Persia, and India brought back with them tales of the exotic creatures that lived in remote mountains and deserts, and in the sea. The world was so wide that any nature of animal seemed possible. The Greek traveler and historian, Herodotus, and Ctesias the Cnidian were the first major chroniclers of these animal marvels. Herodotus wrote of the Phoenix of Arabia, the Giant Ants of India, the Cinnamon Bird, and the Griffins of Scythia. While serving as a physician in the Persian royal court, Ctesias heard tales of the Indian Manticore and the wild Unicorn of India. Their method of describing beasts that people at home had never seen was to compare them to familiar animals.

Early in the Christian era, the Roman Pliny the Elder used this same composite technique in his *Natural History*. The Unicorn, he wrote, has a horselike body, head like a stag, feet like an elephant, tail like a boar, and a single horn. Later authors, accepting the stories of Herodotus, Ctesias, and Pliny, repeated and varied them over the course of two thousand years.

Medieval Beasts

These classical tales were among the animal lore gathered in the *Physiologus* ("The Naturalist" or "The Book of Nature"). Originating near Alexandria between the second and fourth centuries A.D., the collection expanded with Christian allegories and evolved into the medieval bestiaries, which flourished in the twelfth and thirteenth centuries.

While most of the bestiary animals were actual creatures, mixed in with them were the Griffin, Manticore, Crocotta, Phoenix, Basilisk, Salamander, and others from classical literature. Bestiary illuminations of these animals strongly influenced cathedral sculpture and heraldry.

Concurrent with the later bestiaries, popular books of travel spread tales of fantastic animals in exotic lands. *The Romance of Alexander*, *The Travels of Marco Polo*, the voyages of Sinbad the Sailor, and those famous hoaxes, *The Letter of Prester John*, and *The Travels of Sir John Mandeville*, all enriched the body of animal lore.

From Actual to Mythical

Around the time Olaus Magnus produced his 1539 map of Scandinavia, its sea teeming with monstrous creatures, the natural histories of Conrad Gesner and others were raising questions about just how real some beasts were. Edward Topsell's English version of Gesner, *The Historie of Foure-Footed Beastes*, presented traditional fantastic creatures seriously, but the animals' time had come. Sir Thomas Browne denied the existence of many of them in his *Vulgar Errors* (1646)—the beasts could not stand up to rational examination. For the first time in their history, their kind was no longer considered part of the animal kingdom.

The Return of Mythical Beasts

Through the rationalistic eighteenth century and into the nineteenth, the animals were generally dismissed as an embarrassing reminder of human superstition. But renewed interest in the mythic imagination led Western scholars to collect folklore and myths from around the world. Fantastic animals were already there—from the Nagas of India and the Dragons of China and Japan to the Thunderbird of North America. Mythical beasts worldwide spread into scholarly studies then popular culture. Now they are everywhere.

This Book

I modeled this book on the bestiaries of the Middle Ages, but, because it is a book of mythical beasts, I altered the standard bestiary division of Beasts, Birds, Serpents, and Fishes. I added Dragons to the Serpents section and placed it first, owing to the dominance of that age-old, universal beast. Medieval bestiarists loosely ordered the animals in each section according to size or importance, and I, too, use that general arrangement.

One-third of the beasts featured here appeared in the later bestiaries, nearly all deriving in part from classical sources. The other two-thirds of the entries contain myths, legends, and folktales from all over the world. Additional mythical beasts are described in the Micropedia at the back of the book.

I present mythical beasts as bestiaries and natural histories did centuries ago—as though they were actual creatures, members of the animal kingdom. To this end, I have adopted the narrative voice of a modern bestiarist who believes everything he has read about these animals and assumes they are still out there somewhere.

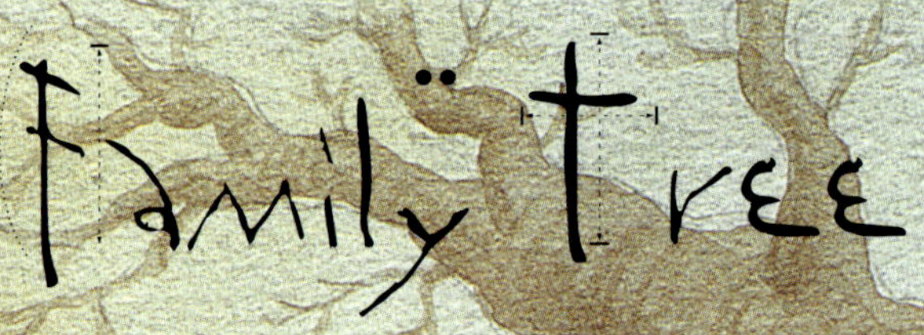

MYTHICAL RELATIVES

Four major families of mythical creatures branch out into groups related by size, shape, and magical powers. Monstrous or beautiful, deadly or beneficent, they all grow from a family tree rooted in the imagination.

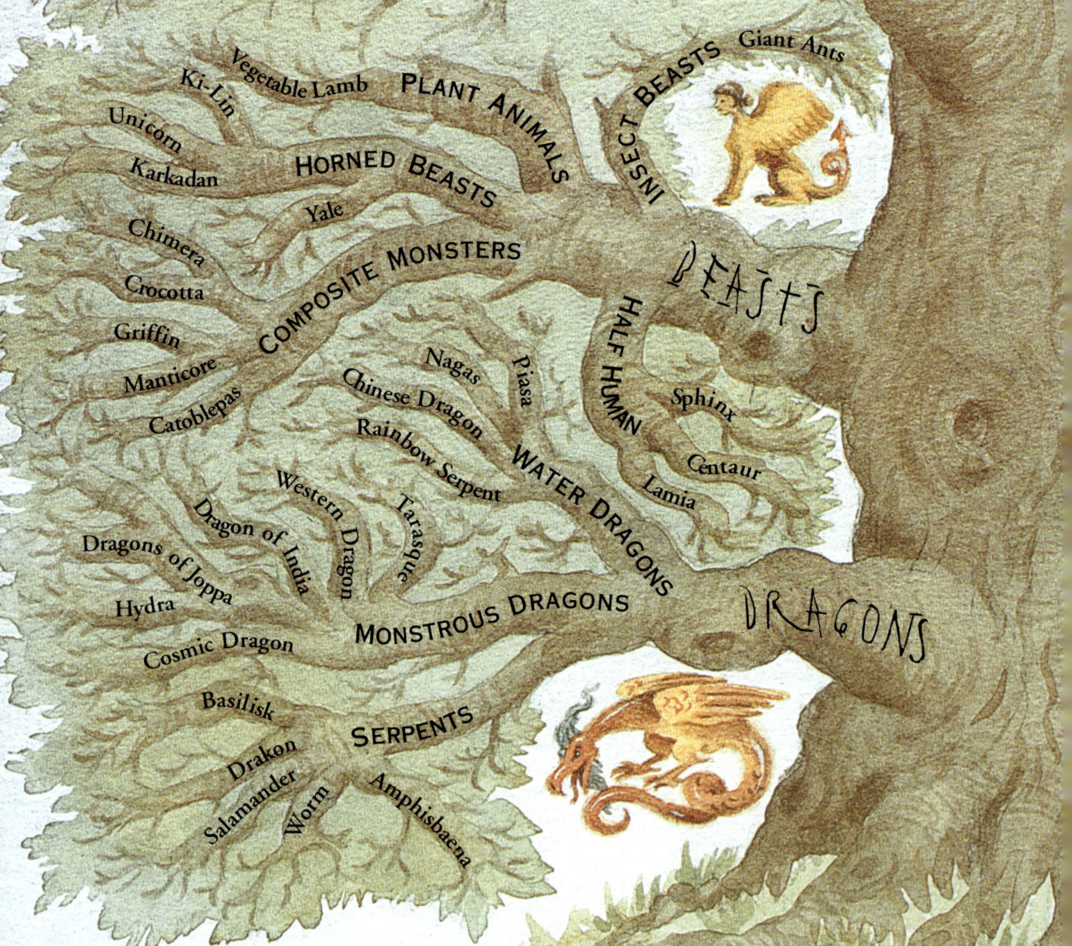

Vegetable Lamb
PLANT ANIMALS
Ki-Lin
Unicorn
Karkadan
HORNED BEASTS
Yale
INSECT BEASTS
Giant Ants
Chimera
Crocotta
Griffin
Manticore
Catoblepas
COMPOSITE MONSTERS
BEASTS
HALF HUMAN
Sphinx
Centaur
Lamia
Nagas
Piasa
Chinese Dragon
Rainbow Serpent
WATER DRAGONS
Western Dragon
Tarasque
Dragon of India
Dragons of Joppa
Hydra
Cosmic Dragon
MONSTROUS DRAGONS
DRAGONS
Basilisk
Drakon
Salamander
Worm
Amphisbaena
SERPENTS

BIRDS

MAJESTIC BIRDS

Benu

Bird of Paradise

Phoenix

Cinnamon Bird

Feng Huang

MONSTROUS BIRDS

Siren

Stymphalids

Peryton

GIGANTIC BIRDS

Roc

Thunderbird

Simurgh

HEALING BIRDS

Caladrius

INSECT BIRDS

Cucuio

PLANT BIRDS

Barnacle Goose

SEA CREATURES

POWERFUL FISH

Remora

LAND-SEA CREATURES

Mermaid

Hippocampus

Bishop Fish

SEA MONSTERS

Aspidochelone

Kraken

Sea Serpent

The World of Mythical Beasts

NORTH AMERICA

1 Mississippi River Valley Thunderbird; Piasa

2 Atlantic Ocean Bishop Fish

CENTRAL AMERICA

3 West Indies Cucuio

EUROPE

4 Throughout the continent Caladrius; Western Dragon

5 Norway Kraken

6 Scotland Barnacle Goose

7 North Atlantic Ocean Aspidochelone; Sea Serpent; Mermaid

8 England Worm

9 Germany Worm

10 France Tarasque

11 Ionian Sea Remora

12 Greece Drakon; Sphinx; Chimera; Hydra; Centaur; Stymphalids

13 Italy Siren

14 Mediterranean Sea Peryton; Hippocampus

ASIA
15 Scythia Griffin
16 Israel Dragons of Joppa
17 Babylonia Cosmic Dragon
18 Arabia Phoenix; Cinnamon Bird
19 Persia Karkadan; Simurgh
20 China Chinese Dragon; Ki-Lin; Feng Huang; Vegetable Lamb
21 India Manticore; Unicorn; Giant Ants; Nagas; Salamander
22 Moluccas Bird of Paradise
5
6
8
4
9
10
11
15
14
13
12
20
24
16
17
19
23
21
18
25
22
26
27
AFRICA
23 Libya Amphisbaena; Lamia
24 Egypt Benu; Sphinx
25 Ethiopia Catoblepas; Crocotta; Yale; Unicorn; Basilisk
26 Madagascar Roc
AUSTRALASIA
27 Australia Rainbow Serpent

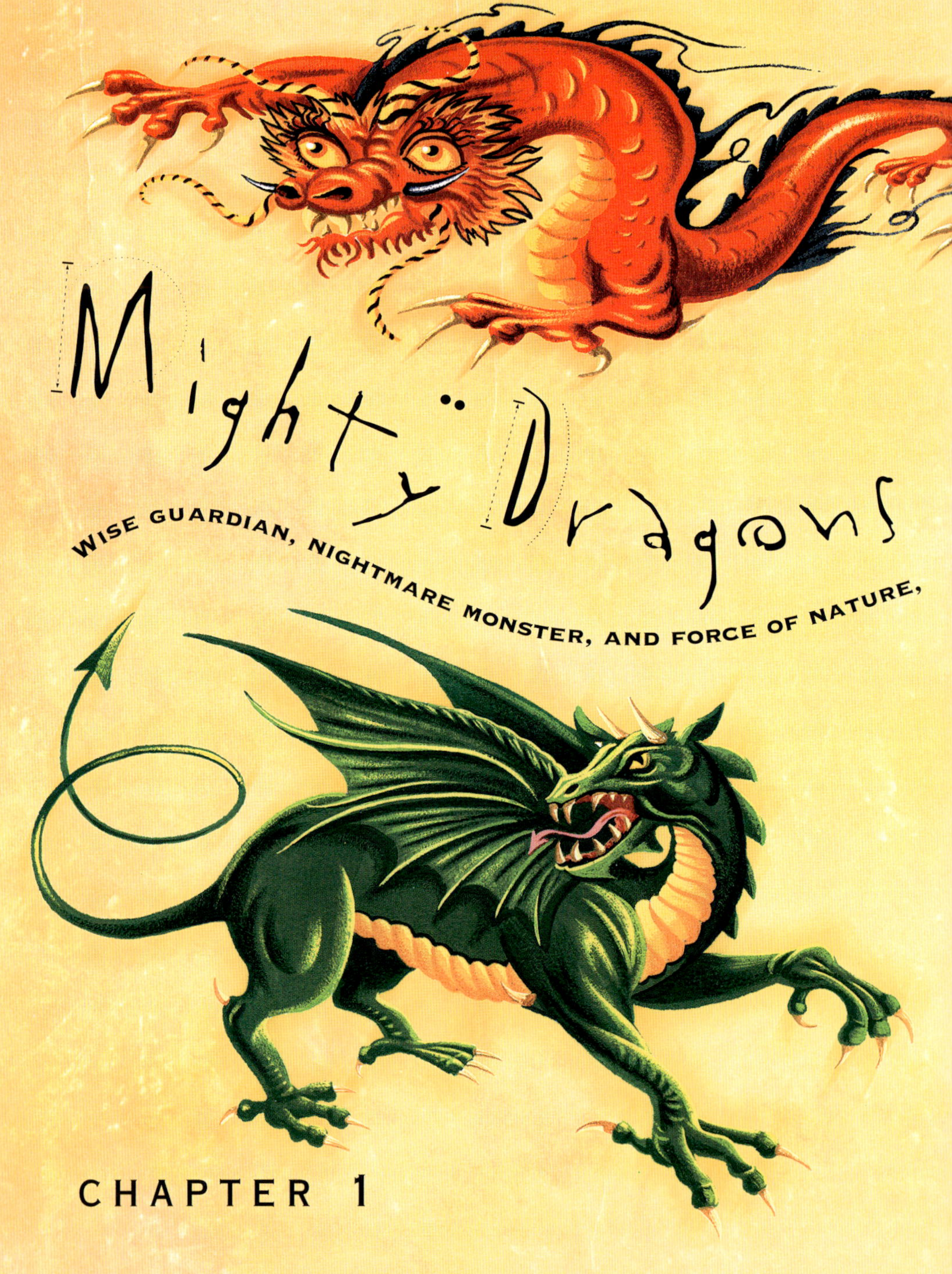
Mighty Dragons
WISE GUARDIAN, NIGHTMARE MONSTER, AND FORCE OF NATURE,
CHAPTER 1

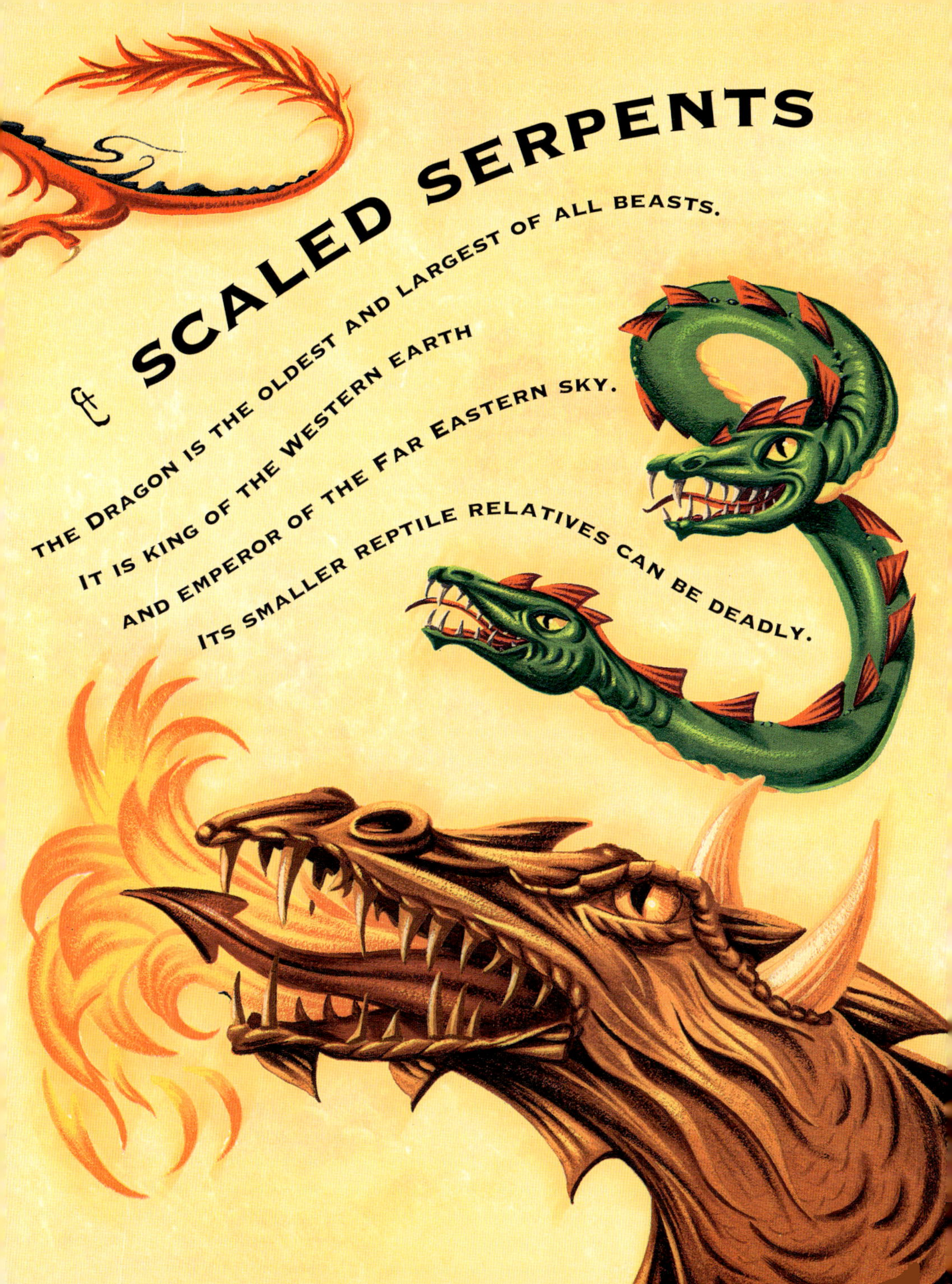

Scaled Serpents

The Dragon is the oldest and largest of all beasts.
It is king of the Western Earth
and emperor of the Far Eastern sky.
Its smaller reptile relatives can be deadly.

Western Dragon

THE KING OF SERPENTS

Largest of all serpents and all the beasts of the earth, the Dragon uncoiled at the beginning of time and has multiplied in names and shapes ever since. Known by all the peoples of the world, it is the greatest of all beasts. In the West, the Dragon is the *drakon* ("sharp-sighted," "watchful") of the Greeks. The Romans call it *draco*, and the British know it as "drake"—as in "firedrake"—and "worm."

The natural historian Edward Topsell says that some Dragons have no feet, some have feet and wings, and some have wings and no feet. Dragons differ from other serpents in having a crest upon their head and a beard under their chin. Their bright eyes see all things. All have teeth. Many have horns or even

The blood of a Dragon is a miraculous elixir that heals grievous wounds

antlers. Some are black with green bellies, some are red, some yellow, and some the color of ash. Many eat poisonous herbs, and their breath infects the air. Many jealously guard treasure deep in the earth.

The best-known kinds of Dragons have either two or four legs. Those with four legs are like the Dragon of Wales. A Dragon with two legs is called a Wyvern. Both of these have scaly bodies that shake the earth when they move. They have broad spiny wings, a barbed tail, and claws and teeth as sharp as blades. They breathe smoke and fire, and their roar alone is enough to make people die of fright. These have battled gods, saints, and knights to the death.

In the head of a Dragon is the Draconce, or Dragon-stone, a brilliant red gem with curative powers. The blood of a Dragon is a miraculous elixir that heals grievous wounds and enables the conqueror of the beast to understand the speech of birds and other living things. When mixed with honey and oil, the fat of the Dragon restores sight.

On old maps, "Here be Dragons" marks unexplored regions on the rims of the world. The dominant monster in heraldry, the Dragon has pointed ears, a barbed tongue, the teeth and scaly stomach of a crocodile, the talons of an eagle, the ribbed wings of a bat, and a barbed, serpentine tail. The beast can be seen nightly as the constellation Draco, which winds across the skies of the northern hemisphere.

Cosmic Dragon

Source of Earth and Sky

The mother of all Dragons was the Babylonian monster, Tiamat. In the beginning, before skies and earth were named, she was the saltwater of the dark primal sea. Only later did she become a Dragoness with a hide so thick that weapons could not pierce it.

Her mate, Apsu, was the freshwater. From the mingling of their waters, Tiamat and Apsu produced pairs of offspring, whose own unruly progeny so annoyed Apsu that he plotted to destroy them. Hearing of his plan, the younger gods bound him with a spell of words and killed him. Incited to vengeance by her older offspring, Tiamat bore all manner of monsters to battle the usurpers: Giant snakes filled with venom, serpents with horns, demons, scorpion-men, fish-men, and bull-men.

A Dragoness with a hide so thick that weapons could not pierce it

With Tiamat's forces assembled to crush them, the younger gods declared Marduk their king and sent him out to do battle with the mother of gods and abominations. Marduk armed himself with a bow, arrows, and a net. He gathered the winds beside him and drove to her in the chariot of a tempest. He ensnared the raging goddess in his net and directed a wind into her face. When she opened her mouth wide to swallow it, the other winds filled her, opening her throat and distending her belly. Marduk shot an arrow straight into her heart. Seeing her fall, her monster hordes scattered. Marduk then split the beast in half. He made half of the body the earth, the other half the sky. He then caught and killed Kingu, her leader of legions, and from his blood created mankind.

The account of the Babylonian Creation was deciphered from cuneiform tablets that a nineteenth-century British archeological team excavated from King Ashurbanipal's library at Nineveh.

Tiamat's Dragon relatives include the Rainbow Serpent of South Africa. Curled around the world with its tail in its mouth, it sleeps at the bottom of the sea.

Chinese Dragon

EMPEROR OF EARTH, SEA, AND SKY

Unlike the evil Dragon of the West, the Dragon of China is a powerful but benevolent ruler of sky, earth, and sea. It is one of the four spiritual animals, a bringer of good fortune, and the founding figure of royal families.

No malignant monster lurking in dark caverns, this Dragon is all rhythmic energy—joyously whirling, twisting, and leaping among the clouds. Horns grow from its horselike head, and long whiskers curve from its bearded muzzle. It has a scaly body and four legs. It often plays with a ball of light as silver as the moon or as gold as the sun. Called a sacred pearl, the globe is thought to be the source of the Dragon's power.

Somewhere in the sky is a jade tablet containing the number of all the Dragons of the East. The Dragons evolve over millennia, beginning as water snakes. All have the power to change their size and shape at will, expanding to cover the sky or shrinking to the size of a worm.

The greatest of the Dragons is the Lung, ruler of the sky. Some say the Lung has the head of a camel, horns of a deer, ears of an ox, eyes of a devil, neck of a snake, belly of a clam, scales of a fish, talons of an eagle, and paws of a tiger. Its voice is like the jangling of copper pans, and its breath forms clouds. Others, too, are weather lords, directing wind, rain, thunder, and lightning. Only when angered do they sink ships or flood villages. Dragon kings in their shining undersea palaces rule the four oceans. Chiao is the supreme Dragon of the earth.

Emperors trace their ancestry back to the five-toed Imperial Dragon. The first Chinese ruler had a Dragon tail, and Dragons pulled the chariots of ancient Emperors.

Dragon figures made of cloth or paper highlight New Year processions, and boats with Dragon-head bows and Dragon-tail sterns race in annual Dragon Boat Festivals.

Dragon figures made of cloth or paper highlight New Year processions

Dragon of India and Ethiopia

SCOURGE OF MARSH AND MOUNTAIN

The Dragon of India and Ethiopia is the largest of all earth Dragons. This creature, among the most long-lived of any animal, grows to a length of 180 feet (55 meters). Its natural enemy is the elephant. Hunters seek the serpent for the mystical gem in its head.

The black Dragon of the marshes is sluggish and has no crest, but the swift Dragon of the mountains has golden scales, a bushy beard, and a tall crest the brightness of fire. The gaze of its deep-set eyes can paralyze an animal or a human being. It has teeth, but its venom is not fatal. It kills with the strength of its tail. Living in the depths of the earth, it makes a sound like clashing brass when it moves. The air shakes when it leaves its den. On stormy nights, four or five of these monsters entwine their tails and fly over the sea.

To satisfy its hunger, the Dragon preys upon the elephant. It lies in wait for the great animal, often in a tree or on a rock, and slides down onto the creature as it passes. The Dragon wraps itself around its victim and tightens its coils until the beast collapses. When the elephant falls onto its attacker, both animals die in the struggle.

Within the Dragon's head is a shining gem that cures all diseases

Within the Dragon's head is a shining gem that cures all diseases. Also, anyone wearing the jewel on the left arm becomes invincible. But the stone retains its power only if it is removed while the serpent is still alive. Hunters place scarlet cloaks embroidered with golden runes outside the Dragon's den. When the Dragon falls under the cloak's spell and crawls outside to sleep, the hunters attack it with axes to acquire its precious jewel. If the animal wakes too soon, it grasps a hunter in its jaws and carries him underground.

The bestiaries say the Dragon is the Devil and its mouth the gates of Hell. Others say this beast of India and Ethiopia is actually the python.

Drakon

GUARDIAN OF SACRED SITES

The sharp-sighted and watchful Drakon of Greece guards sacred springs and treasure. An ancient creature of the earth, it possesses the wisdom of the ages, but anyone trespassing on its hallowed ground does so at his or her own peril.

Oldest and most famous of these large serpents was Python, a she-Dragon born of the mud and slime that remained after the great flood of Deucalion receded. The beast lived beside a spring on the slopes of Parnassus until the god Apollo killed it with his arrows and established his shrine on the spot. This sanctuary became the home of the Delphic Oracle for centuries after, and the god's battle with the monster was ritually reenacted at festivals celebrating the founding of the site.

Anyone trespassing on its hallowed ground does so at his or her own peril

Instructions of the Oracle at Delphi led Cadmus, founder of the city of Thebes, to another spring watched over by another Drakon. This beast had fiery eyes and a forked tongue that flicked among triple rows of teeth. Cadmus crushed the serpent's head with a rock. When he made a sacrifice to Athena, the goddess appeared and told him to sow the Drakon's teeth like seeds. He obeyed and watched as the seeds sprouted into warriors, who fought until only five remained. These five served him in the Theban kingdom that rose from that place.

Athena kept some of the teeth and gave them to Jason for one of the tasks in his quest for the Golden Fleece. Following the demands of King Aeëtes of Colchis in exchange for the Fleece, Jason plowed a field with fire-breathing oxen and scattered the serpent's teeth. Warriors sprang from them and fought, as they had for Cadmus—but this time none survived. The king went back on his word, leading Jason to steal the golden skin, which was guarded by a thousand-coiled Drakon in a sacred grove. Some say Jason battled the serpent, and was swallowed and disgorged. Others say the witch Medea cast a spell upon the creature and, while it slept, Jason took the Fleece from the grove.

Dragons of Joppa

Renowned Beasts of Battle

Among the ancestors of the Dragons of the southern and eastern Mediterranean are two of the most famous monsters of all time. One of these was a beast of the sea, the other a creature of pestilent swamps. Their histories intersect at ancient Joppa, on the coast of Philistia.

The marks of Andromeda's chains can still be seen at Joppa

The older of the two Dragons was Cetus, a beast the god Poseidon called up from the depths of the sea to ravage the country of King Cepheus and Queen Cassiopeia. While waters flooded his lands and Cetus devoured his people, Cepheus learned from an oracle that the only way to stop the destruction was to sacrifice his only daughter, Andromeda, to the monster of the sea. The hero Perseus was flying home on winged sandals after beheading snake-haired Medusa when he saw Andromeda chained to the rock. As the sea beast sped toward the girl, Perseus landed on its back and repeatedly plunged his sword into the scaly hide. Thus did he win a wife and save a kingdom.

Medieval crusaders who fought at Joppa returned home with an account of St. George's battle with the Dragon. George, like Perseus before him, was on a journey when he came upon a maiden in despair. She was the king's daughter, sent to the nearby marsh to appease the Dragon that terrorized the area. When the monster emerged from the murky waters, George attacked it on his steed, driving his lance between its open jaws. The maiden tied her girdle around the neck of the grievously wounded beast and led it into town. George converted the villagers to Christianity and beheaded the monster.

Cetus's skeleton was displayed in Rome, and the marks of Andromeda's chains can still be seen at Joppa. George became the patron saint of England.

Hÿdra

MULTIHEADED TERROR OF HEAVEN AND EARTH

The monstrous Hydra (Greek for "water serpent") is a Dragon with many heads. As soon as one of the heads is destroyed, others grow in its place.

Most famous of these hideous beasts was the Hydra of Lerna, one of the many abominations spawned by Echidna and Typhon. This Hydra lived in the marshes, poisoning the air with its breath and laying waste to the countryside. Like something out of a nightmare, it had many heads, each waving like a separate serpent. Some say the creature had fifty heads, others a hundred, and still others a thousand, but most say nine. When one head was destroyed, two or three more would grow in its place. One of the heads, made of gold, was immortal.

This was the monster that King Eurystheus sent Hercules to slay for the second of his Twelve Labors. Hercules set upon the Hydra with his club but for every head he crushed others rose to strike him. In desperation, he appealed for aid from his charioteer, Iolaus. The friend came to his side with burning brands and when Hercules severed a head, Iolaus seared its stump with fire. No new heads grew. Hercules severed the final, immortal head with his sword and buried it under a boulder, where it still hisses to this day.

As soon as one of the heads is destroyed others grow in its place

One of the Hydra's many relatives was the great red Dragon of the Apocalypse. This form of Satan had seven heads and ten horns, and each head bore a crown. St. Michael and his angels fought the Old Serpent and its angels and cast them out of Heaven and into the bottomless pit. Other relatives of the Hydra include the many-headed Scylla and the Dragon that guarded the Golden Apples of the Hesperides.

Hydra is the genus of freshwater polyps, whose many arms, some say, resemble the monster's serpentine necks. The Hydra, or Seven-Headed Dragon, is also a heraldic crest.

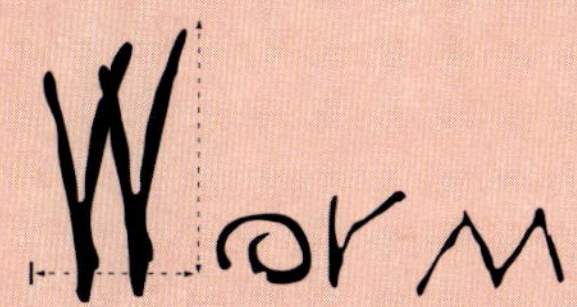

Ward of Ancient Treasure

Widespread in the northern countries, the Worm (Wurm, Wyrm) is one of the most fearsome of Dragons. It lives deep in the earth, jealously guarding age-old gems and gold. Vast in size, this monster is covered with scales as hard as steel. Fangs, fire, and claws protect its soft throat and underbelly. Others of its kind coil themselves around hills. Both devastate the countryside, striking terror into the hearts of all.

It lives deep in the earth jealously guarding age-old gems and gold

Best known of the early Worms was the nemesis of the warrior-king Beowulf. This Dragon guarded a treasure hoard for hundreds of years before a slave slipped into its lair while it slept and made off with a jeweled cup. After the Worm wreaked its fiery vengeance on the people of that land, the aging king confronted the Dragon at its barrow. The Dragon advanced, hurling fire at the iron shield. Beowulf's sword rang against the beast's scales. When the infuriated monster breathed another torrent of flame, Prince Wiglaf came to the aid of the old warrior. He thrust his sword into the Worm's neck, and Beowulf split its chest with his dagger. Beast and hero died together. Wiglaf buried the Dragon's treasure in the funeral mound of his king.

Germanic Siegfried (Sigurd), too, knew Dragon battle. Urged by the devious dwarf, Regin, the young hero set out to destroy Fafnir, guardian of the cursed Ring of the Nibelungs. Siegfried hid in a pit outside the creature's cave and, when the monster emerged, the warrior plunged his blade up into the soft stomach. While cooking the Dragon's heart for Regin, Siegfried tasted the blood of the beast and understood the speech of birds.

Another way to slay Worms is with spiked armor such as the Heir of Lambton wore when he met the Lambton Worm in the River Wear. More of More Hall was equipped with similar armor when he slew the Dragon of Wantley. Worm Hill, in England, is a mound whose ridges, some say, were formed by the coils of the Lambton Worm.

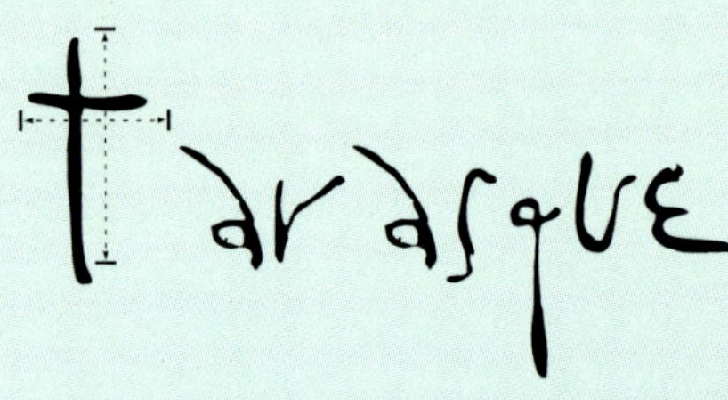

SPIKE-BACKED RIVER MONSTER

The Dragon called Tarasque is the bane of the Rhône Valley in southern France. Larger than an ox, this monster has six mighty legs, the head of a lion, paws of a bear, and a scaly body with a long serpentine tail ending in a barb as sharp as a spear's point. The hard, leathery shell on its back is covered with spikes. The spikes of a vanquished Tarasque can be attached to knights' armor.

The best known of these hideous creatures lurked in the river beside the town of Nerluc. It sank ships on the Rhône and devoured their crews. It killed travelers in the dark forest surrounding the town. And then it entered Nerluc itself and carried off townspeople. Survivors entreated St. Martha to come to their aid, because she was the one who had converted the people to the Catholic faith. She entered the woods alone in search of the beast. When she at last came upon it, guided by its roars, it was engorging yet another victim. Martha approached the brute, her crucifix upheld, and sprinkled it with holy water. It dropped its prey and stood quietly while she tied her belt around its neck. She led the docile creature into town and the people killed it with stones and spears.

The villagers named the monster Tarasque and changed the name of their town from Nerluc to Tarascon in honor of their victory. One can still see a Tarasque on the streets of Tarascon, as a comic figure in festival processions. With a young "St. Martha" leading it by a cord, a cloth monster with movable head and tail and human feet lumbers harmlessly through the town.

The spikes of a vanquished Tarasque can be attached to knights' armor

Another saint, Margaret, is famous for subduing a Dragon relative of the Tarasque. After refusing to marry the governor of Antioch, she was tortured and thrown into a prison cell, where a hideous Dragon appeared before her. As it advanced to devour her, she made the sign of the cross. The beast vanished into thin air. In another version of the tale, the Dragon swallowed her whole. By the power of the cross, the creature burst open and the virgin emerged unharmed.

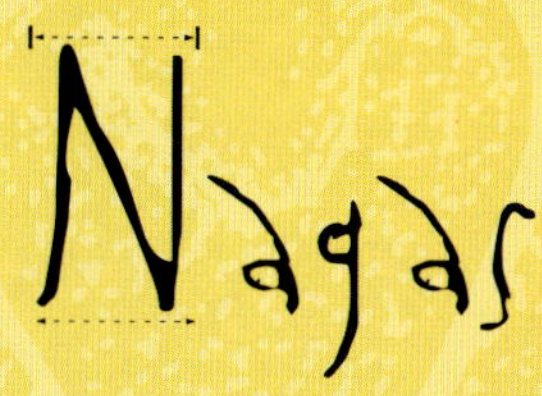

SERPENTS OF THE WATERS

The Nagas of India are Dragons of the earth, waters, sky, and the heavens. These creatures take on different forms. Some are all serpent, with many heads. Some have the heads or upper bodies of humans and lower bodies of serpents, and yet others resemble humans with snakes crowning their heads or growing from their necks.

Hidden Nagas are guardians of treasure deep within the earth. The underground capital of these creatures is Bhogavati, a glittering city of flowers and music, ruled by the snake-king Takshaka. Nagas of the waters live in springs, rivers, and lakes, and have palaces of gold, rubies, and emeralds at the bottom of the sea. Divine Nagas of the sky form clouds and produce fertile rain, but when angered they devastate the earth with floods. Heavenly Nagas guard the temples of the gods. When Nagas leave their homes, they become the prey of their enemy, the gigantic Garuda bird.

Nagas are said to possess a divine pearl of knowledge within their coils. Both beneficent and destructive, they give rubies to human beings who win their favor, but their venom is deadly.

At the Creation and in periods of rest, Vishnu sleeps on the King of the Nagas, Sesha, whose body forms the bed and whose hooded heads arch over the god as a protecting canopy.

Nagas that caused rain to fall were once captured and placed in a box. Their confinement led to seven years of drought. Others were conquered by a king of Nepal. They drew likenesses of themselves with their own blood and presented them to the king, saying that veneration of the pictures would lead to rain.

Sculpted figures of Nagas guard doorways of sacred places, and stone slabs inscribed with their image are placed on platforms around Asvattha trees to assure human fertility.

In their powers to control the weather, Nagas are related to the Dragons of China and the Rainbow Serpent.

they give rubies to human beings who win their favor

Rainbow Serpent

DRAGON OF RAIN AND RIVERS

Striped with all the colors of earth and sky, the enormous Rainbow Serpent is the most beautiful of all the Dragons. One of its kind lives in the ocean and, when it moves, waves begin to roll. Others live in the earth or in ponds and rivers. During rainy seasons, they rise up to drink the moisture in the air, and then bend back down to the ground to drink the water of the earth. These shining creatures can be seen all around the world.

In the Australian Dreamtime, when the world was new and the Ancestors created and named all living things, the Rainbow Serpent crawled through the land, carving out rivers and forming mountains. It rested by curling up in a lake, and, while it slept, drought spread across the earth. One of the Ancestors disturbed the monster while fishing at the lake. The beast rose up in a rage, sending water spilling out of the lake and flooding the plain. Rain poured from the sky, raising the waters even more. And so did the Rainbow Serpent cause the Great Flood. Now, when a shaman sits beside a pool where the serpent lives and is filled with its spirit, he or she gains powers to cure sickness and foretell the future.

When a shaman sits beside a serpent's pool, he or she gains powers to cure sickness and foretell the future

The Rainbow Serpent of West Africa was the first creature made by the creator god Mawu. The serpent carried the god on its back as it crawled across the land, its waving tracks forming the bends of riverbeds. When its journey was done, the Dragon curled up in the bottom of the sea, its tail in its mouth, supporting the world. Its relatives include the ancient Ouroboros and the extinct Midgard Serpent of Scandinavia.

Associated with rain and fertility, the Rainbow Serpent is related to the Rain Dragons of China. In times of drought, the ancient Chinese made Dragons of wood and paper and carried them in processions. If no rain followed, they destroyed the Dragons.

Piasa

The Horned River Serpent

Fishermen and travelers from the Mississippi Valley to the Great Lakes are warned to avoid any Piasa painted or carved on cliffs

Living along the Mississippi River in North America, the Piasa (pronounced *pie*-a-saw) is a Dragon that the Algonquin-speaking peoples call "the bird that devours men."

The Piasa is a hideous beast with the face of an angry man, sharp teeth, the beard of a tiger, the antlers of a deer, spiny wings, a scaly body, and four bird legs with the talons of an eagle. Wrapped over its body is a long scorpionlike tail that ends in the fluke of a fish. It carries off deer and men.

When the French missionaries Jacques Marquette and Louis Joliet were exploring the great Mississippi, they came upon huge figures of the Piasa painted on the cliffs above a turbulent stretch of water. The painted rocks have since been quarried away, but the monster has been painted on a bluff outside Alton, Illinois. Now a tourist attraction, the Piasa glares menacingly from postcards and T-shirts.

Fishermen and travelers from the Mississippi Valley to the Great Lakes are warned to avoid any Piasa painted or carved on cliffs. Beneath it is dangerous water, with whirlpools and rapids.

Close relatives of the antlered Piasa is the Horned Serpent, found throughout North America, and the giant water reptile of Tennessee and the Carolinas, the winged Uktena. A priceless gem shines upon its head, but that stone is never taken, because the monster's breath alone kills humans and other living creatures.

Some Horned Serpents have one red horn and one green. They live in deep water and swallow anyone who comes near. When captured—which is rarely—their bodies are burned, leaving only the living heart, which is used as medicine. The Horned Serpent is the enemy of the Thunderbird. When the two battle, the sky shakes, lightning shoots like arrows, and rain pours down upon the earth.

Basilisk

Lethal King of Snakes

Born from the blood of the Gorgon's eyes, the Basilisk is the deadly king of small serpents. On its forehead is a white mark resembling a crown. Although this beast is less than a foot (30 centimeters) long, the lethal stare of its red eyes shrivels the largest snake or any other living being that looks upon it. Its toxic breath withers forests into deserts, splits rocks, and poisons streams. Birds flying overhead drop dead from its stench.

The little monster's venom is so powerful that if the creature bites an item in someone's hand, that person dies. As one story goes, the poison in a Basilisk that was wounded by a knight traveled up the horseman's spear, killing both the rider and the horse.

But no creature is without its match. The monster's natural enemy is the weasel. When a weasel enters the lair of a Basilisk, the serpent flees, but the weasel pursues and kills it. Another animal fatal to the Basilisk is the cock, whose crowing sends the beast into convulsions until it dies. This is why travelers on the Libyan desert always take roosters with them, assuring their safe passage.

And there is yet another way to destroy a Basilisk, as the great Alexander did. When besieging a certain city, many of his warriors died without a wound. Seeking the cause of the mysterious deaths, the army discovered a Basilisk upon the city wall and knew it was the beast's malignant gaze that had killed their comrades. Alexander commanded that a mirror be placed between the army and the Basilisk. Upon seeing its own image reflected in the mirror, the monster died instantly.

St. George, also, turned his shield so that the Basilisk expired when it beheld its own shape.

Basilisk ashes can be scattered in temples to prevent venomous spiders from weaving their webs inside. The Basilisk's closest relative is the Cockatrice, a winged reptile with legs and a rooster crest. It is born of a cock's egg and hatched by a toad.

Basilisk ashes can be scattered in temples to prevent venomous spiders from weaving their webs inside

Amphisbaena

The Dragon With Two Heads

The Amphisbaena (Greek for "goes both ways") is a Dragon with a head at each end of its body. It is one of the deadly serpents spawned by the blood of the Gorgon Medusa after wing-footed Perseus carried her dripping head over the Libyan desert.

Amphisbaena skin is a remedy for chilblains. reducing the swelling of hands and feet inflamed by cold

The two heads of the Amphisbaena are the same size as the rest of its body. While one head sleeps, the other remains watchful, its eyes bright as fire. With the second head where its tail should be, the swift creature can attack prey or elude capture by going either forward or backward. When both heads move forward, the serpent forms a circle. Or, grasping one head in its other mouth, it can roll like a hoop. The excruciating poison of its bite quickly kills its victim.

Amphisbaena skin is a remedy for chilblains, reducing the swelling of hands and feet inflamed by cold. *Amphisbaena* is the scientific name for a genus of legless worm lizards that can move both ways and can lift their tails to make them look like heads.

The Amphisbaena is now widespread, sharing its desert home with other serpents that lie in wait for the unwary animal or traveler.

The Jaculus is so named because it is like a javelin. It hides in barren trees, and when man or beast approaches, it coils itself up like a spring and shoots its body at its prey.

The Scytale is an indolent serpent. It is too sluggish to chase its victim but its markings are so beautiful that anyone looking at them is transfixed. This creature's poison is so fiery that anyone it bites literally burns up in flames. The Scytale sheds its skin in winter.

The Seps is not a large snake but its venom destroys the bones and the body.

The Dipsa is so small that someone can step on it without seeing it, and its bite so painless that the victim is unaware that he or she is about to die as the poison takes its toll.

Salamander

Denizen of Fire

A small four-footed Dragon, the Salamander is mighty beyond its size. This spotted lizardlike beast is so cold it extinguishes flames at will, and produces "Salamander's Wool," a magical fire-resistant fabric. It is one of the deadliest of animals and destroys entire villages with its poison.

This creature is found near fire. In seeking out the hottest flames, it crawls into the forges of blacksmiths. When the flames lower and the fire dies, smiths know a Salamander is in the shop. They must hunt it out and destroy it before the forge can be rekindled.

The Salamander is also seen around the foot of volcanoes, living in the heat of the flowing lava. There is such a mountain in the Kingdom of Prester John, King of all the Indias. Salamanders in the flames spin a silky thread that can be woven into fine garments. Instead of being washed, clothing made of Salamander's Wool is placed back in the fire. When it is removed from the flames, it is as clean as when it was first made.

Salamanders in the flames spin a silky thread that can be woven into fine garments

Salamander cloth also comes from the Chinese province of Chingintalas. This fabric is made from minerals taken from the earth and pounded into fibers. Cloth of this kind was produced for the Great Khan of China.

Marco Polo argued that "Salamander" was thus a substance, not an animal.

The Salamander exudes a milky liquid from its skin and mouth. Anyone touching the foul matter loses his or her hair, and the contaminated flesh discolors and breaks out in a rash. When the Salamander climbs a tree, its poison infects the fruit and kills all who eat it. And when the serpent falls into a well, it spreads deadly disease to everyone who drinks the water. If a pig eats a Salamander, the pig remains healthy, but anyone eating the pig dies.

To the alchemists, the Salamander is the spirit of fire, an essential agent in transforming base metals into gold. In heraldry, the figure is depicted in flames, representing courage that cannot be consumed by adversity.

CHAPTER 2

FOUR-LEGGED Beasts

WITH FOUR LEGS OR MORE, THESE RARE CREATURES ROAM THE REMOTE PLACES OF THE EARTH.

ADVENTURERS WHO SEEK MAGICAL HORNS AND CLAWS MUST BE WARY OF PARALYZING GAZES, FIERY BREATH, AND SPIKES FROM SCORPION TAILS.

Griffin

Beast of Magical Powers

With the body and hind legs of the lion, King of Beasts, and the wings, forefeet, and head of the eagle, Monarch of the Air, the Griffin is the most majestic of all beasts. Its eyes are as bright as fire, and its talons are as large as the horns of an ox. This creature of two worlds is so strong it can carry off its mortal enemy, the horse.

Named from the Greek *gryps*, meaning "curved, curled, having a hooked nose," Griffins roam the wild regions of the earth. In the Hyperborean mountains of Scythia, they dig up gold and emeralds with their talons and build nests of these treasures in the rocky cliffs. The one-eyed men of that country, called Arimaspi, wage constant war on the creatures, attempting to steal the gold to adorn their hair. The Griffins of India also live in remote mountains rich with ore. The bravest of the local warriors will raid the beasts' domain on moonless nights to dig up the precious metal. Few are fortunate enough to escape both with their lives and with treasure.

It is said that a drinking vessel fashioned from a Griffin claw will change color in the presence of poison. A Griffin's feather, passed over the eyes of the blind, can restore sight.

The Griffin comes from a long line of guardians and protectors. The first of their kind appeared in Mesopotamia and Egypt about five thousand years ago in the company of deities and kings. In Egypt, with the head of the Sacred Hawk, they conquered the enemies of the Pharaoh. A pair of them reclined on either side of the Cretan ruler in the Palace of Minos. The beasts pulled Apollo's chariot of the sun and once carried Alexander the Great aloft in a basket so that he could explore the sky.

The Griffin's closest relative is the Hippogriff. Others in the family tree include the Roc and the Simurgh.

A Griffin's feather passed over the eyes of the blind can restore sight

Unicorn

MYSTERIOUS CREATURE WITH A SPIRAL HORN

Solitary and wild, the Unicorn is the most elusive of nature's creatures. Prized for the medicinal uses of its magical horn, this animal is often hunted but seldom slain, and is even more rarely captured alive.

The early Unicorn of India was a fierce beast as large as a horse. It was a solid-hoofed animal with a white body, a dark red head, and blue eyes. Its tapered horn was mostly white but black in the middle, and ended in a sharp point of bright crimson. The animal was so strong and swift that the only way hunters could catch it was to surround it when it was with its foals. Refusing to leave its young, the Unicorn defended them from the hunters with its life. So says Ctesias the Cnidian. This beast was often confused with the rhinoceros.

A different kind of Unicorn is a beautiful, gentle creature. It is smaller in size, all white, with a goatlike beard, slender legs, cloven hooves, and a long, graceful horn spiraling from its forehead. It is thought to have been one of the animals in the Garden of Eden. This magical animal purifies poisonous waters with its horn. It is captured only by a virgin who lures it to her with her innocent charm. The subdued animal is then killed or led off to the king's palace.

The object of the hunt has always been the precious horn, called "alicorn." One can fashion Unicorn horns into cups, or make potions of powdered horn, to counteract poison and prevent disease. Its curative powers make alicorn worth its weight in gold. Unscrupulous merchants sell horns of other animals as alicorn. To test if powdered horn is actually from a Unicorn, the customer arranges it into a circle on a flat surface and places a spider within the circle. If the spider does not crawl out of the circle, the horn is considered genuine.

The Unicorn has been portrayed in art since ancient times: on Mesopotamian cylinder seals, in bestiaries, on medieval tapestries, and in Renaissance paintings. Monoceros, also known as the Unicorn, is a constellation in the northern sky.

One can fashion Unicorn horns into cups or make potions of powdered horn to counteract poison and prevent disease

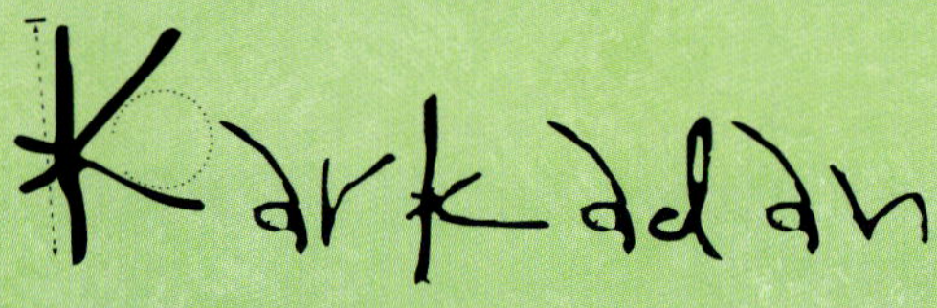

Karkadan

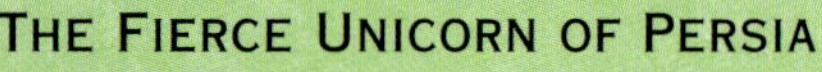

THE FIERCE UNICORN OF PERSIA

The bull-like Karkadan has a long, curved horn growing from its forehead. This monster's horn is so deadly, its breath so vile, and its bellow so thunderous that it strikes terror in most living creatures.

Among the beasts, only the elephant stands its ground against the Karkadan. To defeat this enemy, the one-horned creature must avoid the coiling trunk that can lift even a Karkadan into the air and dash it to the ground. It attacks the elephant from underneath, thrusting its horn into the creature's belly. But, as the dead elephant's fat flows down over the horn, it blinds the Karkadan, making both creatures easy prey for the giant Roc. Seizing the joined beasts in its talons, the bird flies off to feed them to its young. So says Sinbad the Sailor.

Karkadan horn is made into knife handles that sweat in the presence of poison

The Persian hero Iskandar, known in the West as Alexander the Great, is said to be the first man to tame a Karkadan. As one story goes, the future conqueror of the world was in his teens when a Karkadan was presented to his father, Philip of Macedon, as a gift. Philip offered the animal and a prize of gold to anyone who could ride it. Others tried in vain, attempting to overpower the animal, but, when Iskandar spoke to it gently, it knelt before him in submission. Western tales, too, sometimes present Alexander's horse, Bucephalus, as a Unicorn.

The less violent side of the Karkadan's nature is also evoked by the ringdove. The beast will lie contentedly for hours, delighting in the bird's song.

The Persians attempt to capture the Karkadan in the same way Europeans hunt the Unicorn: by persuading a fair virgin to lure the creature to her lap. When the animal succumbs to her wiles, the hunters encircle it and kill it with their spears.

In rare instances, a live Karkadan, outwitted by its animal prey, has been found with its horn deeply imbedded in a tree. Karkadan horn is made into knife handles that sweat in the presence of poison.

Ki-Lin

Ethereal Herald

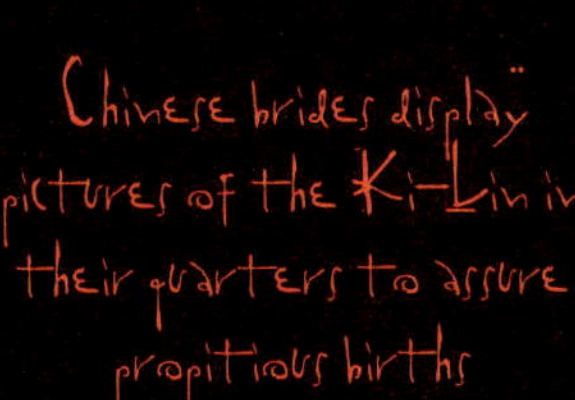

One of the four auspicious animals of China, the Ki-Lin is king of the 360 beasts of the earth. It has the body of a stag, the tail of an ox, the hooves of a horse, and a long fleshy horn growing from its forehead. Its body is bright with the five sacred colors—red, yellow, blue, white, and black—and its voice is like a monastery bell. A gentle creature, it will not tread upon insects or eat living grass.

The Ki-Lin (Kilin, Qilin) embodies both male (Ki) and female (Lin) powers. Born in the center of the earth, it lives beyond the clouds, appearing to mankind only to presage the birth of a great person, to herald the reign of a benevolent Emperor, or to foretell a ruler's impending death.

Legend has it that five thousand years ago, the Emperor Fu Hsi was sitting on a river bank when the creature suddenly materialized beside him. On its back were magical symbols that he traced on the ground with a stick. These signs, it is said, formed the beginning of the written language of China.

Of all the Ki-Lin's omens, the most widely known is the creature's appearance to the mother of Confucius only months before the sage was born. In its mouth it carried a jade tablet upon which were engraved characters prophesying: "The son of mountain crystal will rule as a throneless king." The astonished young woman took a ribbon from her hair and tied it to the Ki-Lin's horn. In his old age, Confucius came upon a Ki-Lin wounded by hunters. Seeing his mother's ribbon on its horn, he knew his death was imminent. Ever since, Chinese brides have displayed pictures of the Ki-Lin in their quarters to assure propitious births.

Other varieties of Chinese Unicorns include the Kioh Twan, the Poh, the Hiai Chai, and the Too Jon Sheu.

Sphinx

CREATURE OF MYSTERY AND RIDDLES

The Sphinx (from Greek, "to bind tight," "strangle") is an enigmatic creature whose name is given to three different kinds of beasts. Those with bodies of lions and heads of human beings came from Egypt and Greece, while an apelike monster, described by writers of natural history, roams in Ethiopia and India.

She stopped all travelers and asked them a question. Those who could not answer the riddle she strangled and devoured

Oldest of these is the animal form of the Egyptian pharaoh, with the body of the King of Beasts and the head of the human king. A colossal figure of this royal beast guards the Pyramids of Giza. Cut out of stone, the Great Sphinx is 240 feet (73 meters) long and nearly 70 feet (21 meters) high. Other Egyptian Sphinxes have the head of a ram (Criosphinx) or a falcon (Hierocosphinx). Most Egyptian Sphinxes are male.

The Sphinxes of Greece are female. The first of its kind was one of the monstrous brood of the nymph-snake Echidna who also bore the Hydra of Lerna and the fire-breathing Chimera. Most renowned of this Sphinx's descendants was the dreaded creature that the gods sent from Ethiopia to punish Thebes. She was lion-bodied with female breasts, a woman's head, wings of an eagle, and the tail of a serpent. Crouched on a cliff outside the city, she stopped all travelers and asked them a question: "What has four legs, two legs, and three legs, and the more legs it has the weaker it is?" She strangled and devoured those who could not answer the riddle. Only one traveler ever matched her wits. It was Oedipus, future king of Thebes. The answer, he said, was man, who crawls as a baby, walks as a youth and man, and uses a cane in old age. Defeated, the Sphinx hurled herself off the rock to her death.

Roman authors and others since have used the name Sphinx (or Sphinga) for an apelike animal living in the wilds of Ethiopia and India. This beast has coarse brown hair and breasts like a woman. Its voice is similar to a human's but is unintelligible.

Chimera

LION, GOAT, AND SERPENT

It gave its name to any composite monster and to absurd ideas and wild fancies

One of a kind, the Chimera (Greek for "she-goat") was a fire-breathing monster with the powers of three beasts. It had the head and foreparts of a lion, the body of a goat, and the hindquarters of a dragon. Some say that besides its lion's head, the head of a goat grew from its back, and its tail ended in the head of a serpent.

This creature was one of the grotesque offspring of the snake-woman Echidna and Typhon, spirit of hurricanes. From its cave in the Asia Minor kingdom of Lycia, it ravaged the countryside until the king gave the hero Bellerophon the task of slaying the menace. Not knowing how to accomplish this daunting feat, the youth consulted a seer, who told him victory would be his if he rode the winged horse Pegasus.

The immortal horse had sprung from the blood of the severed head of snake-haired Medusa, who died at the hand of Perseus. Pegasus lived on the slopes of Mount Helicon, home of the Muses, where it created the divine spring Helicon by pawing at the earth. The horse was asleep on the ground when Bellerophon slipped a magical golden bridle over its head, given to him by the goddess Athena.

Tamed by the divine gift, Pegasus carried Bellerophon through the sky to the Chimera's lair. The beast breathed fire as the horse winged down upon it and Bellerophon thrust a lead-tipped spear between the gaping jaws. Melting in the heat, the lead flowed through the body of the monster, killing it on the spot.

Some think the Chimera is a volcano of the same name, with lions living at its fiery summit, goats grazing on its green slopes, and serpents writhing at its rocky base. While the Chimera was the only one of its kind, it gave its name to any composite monster and to absurd ideas and wild fancies. The Chimera's closest Far Eastern relative is the Bixie of China, a lion with horns and wings.

Lamia

DEADLY BEAST OF THE DESERT

> With the sweetness of its voice it draws desert travelers near and then to their death

A monster of the Libyan desert, the Lamia devours children and lures men to their doom.

The best-known creature of this kind is a four-footed beast with the head and breasts of a woman, a scaly, dragonlike body, and a long horselike tail. Its forefeet clawed like a bear's and its hind feet cloven like a goat's, this Lamia is said to be one of the swiftest of all creatures, able to run down any prey. It also kills by deceit. With the sweetness of its voice, it draws desert travelers near—and then to their death. The beast also travels to the sea at the edge of the desert and lies in wait to attack shipwrecked sailors who wander ashore.

The first Lamia was a beautiful woman beloved of Zeus, and by whom she bore many children. Enraged with jealousy, the goddess Hera slew the young engendered by her divine husband. Unable to avenge herself on the gods, Lamia, in turn, killed mortal children. Her face became hideous and nightmarish. She could pluck out her own eyes and place them back in their sockets.

Other Lamia, assuming the shape of human women, are renowned for enticing young men to lie with them—and then sucking their blood. But they are not always successful. Disguising herself as a fair maiden, one Lamia met a Greek youth traveling to Corinth. She told him that, if he would go home with her, she would sing for him, give him rare wine, and live with him for all their days. The young man could not resist. At their wedding feast, the mystic Apollonius recognized her true Lamia nature and made her confess that she, her house, and all that was in it were illusions conjured up by her demonic powers. She wept at being revealed—and then she and her insubstantial shapes vanished into thin air.

Other Lamia are in the shape of women above the waist and serpents below. These, along with their equally deadly sisters, are related to the Siren and the Mermaid.

Centaur

HORSE-MAN OF THESSALY

A savage but wise being, the Centaur is a horse-man—a man from the waist up, with the legs, body, and tail of a horse. The animal and human natures of this creature tend to be at war with each other, making it unpredictably violent or benevolent. It lives in the mountains of Thessaly.

Centaurs are said to descend from Ixion, son of the king of the Lapiths, and a cloud in the likeness of the goddess Hera. Their son, Centaurus, mated with mares, spawning the barbarous horse-men of the mountains. These beasts are best known for their battle with the civilized Lapiths. In one tale, the Centaurs, invited to a royal wedding feast, became wild with wine and attempted to carry off the bride.

The animal and human natures of this creature tend to be at war with each other making it unpredictably violent or benevolent

Later Centaurs were ruled by Chiron, who was known for his goodness and wisdom and was skilled in the arts of music, medicine, and archery. Chiron became the tutor of Achilles, Hercules, and other heroes. Hercules accidentally killed the benign creature with a poisoned arrow during a skirmish with the Centaurs. Years later, Hercules met his own end through the deception of the Centaur Nessus, whose "gift" of a poisoned shirt stuck to the hero's body and burned him to death.

Some mistakenly think Centaurs derive from the Thessalonians, the first men Greeks ever saw riding horses. The natives of Mexico, too, considered Spanish soldiers and their mounts to be a single animal.

Chiron is immortalized in the archer sign of a zodiacal constellation, and the constellation Centaurus appears in the southern sky. The Centaur is also a heraldic figure.

The Centaur's closest relative is the Onacentaur (the Ass-Centaur), a shaggy beast whose humanlike face and torso is covered with coarse hair. More distant relatives include the Deer-Centaur, the Dog-Centaur, and even the half-human, half-goat Satyr.

Manticore

Scorpion Tail With a Human Face

The Manticore (Mardkhora, Martichoras) is one of the most feared of wild beasts. Its name derives from Old Persian, meaning "man-eater."

This monster is the size of the largest lion, with shaggy fur as red as cinnabar. Its eyes are blue. It has the face and ears of a man, but in its mouth are three rows of teeth, suitable for ripping flesh. Lethal stings crown its head and bristle from its scorpionlike tail. It is swift and so powerful it can leap over any obstacle. Its deceptively pleasing voice resembles the sounds of a panpipe and a trumpet.

The Manticore terrifies other animals, and it delights in devouring human flesh. It lies in wait for humans—preferring two or three at a time—and attacks them with the poisonous stings on its tail. The shafts are a forearm long, as thin as fine thread, and travel as though shot from a bow. The Manticore can shoot its fatal spikes either forward or backward. It can curve its tail over its body and cast the darts over its head, or it can straighten its tail and hurl the stings straight behind it. As soon as the arrows leave the tail, others spring out to replace them.

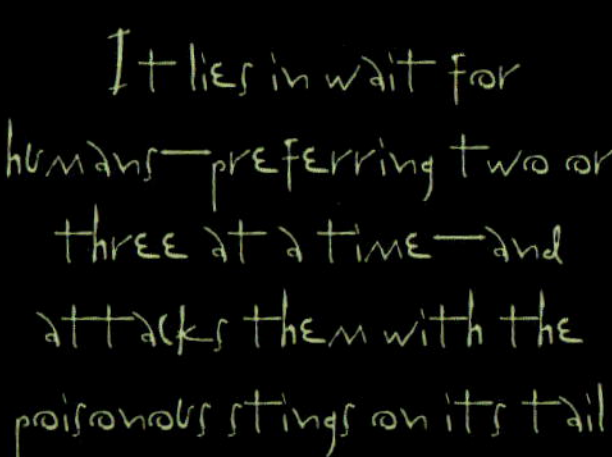

The only creature that can survive the stings is the elephant, which is why hunters ride those gentle beasts when attacking the Manticore with arrows.

The first to describe the Manticore was Ctesias the Cnidian, who said he saw such a creature when it was brought from India as a gift to the King of Persia. Ctesias has been credited ever after with making this deadly beast known to the world.

Some think the monster is a Bengal tiger, appearing red in color as it runs through sunlight. They say that the three rows of teeth and the scorpionlike spikes were fanciful details born of the terror felt by those who told Ctesias the tale.

Yale

THE BEAST WITH MOVABLE HORNS

One of the many strange animals of Ethiopia and India, the Yale (Eale, Jall) is remarkable for its horns. This creature is tawny or black, is the size of a horse, and has the tail of an elephant, the jaws of a boar, and long, sharp horns that it can move at will.

When the Yale is attacked by man or beast, it points one of the horns forward like a lance and swivels the other back out of harm's way. If the thrusting horn is damaged in the battle, it turns backward and the second horn rises to take its place. Some say the horns are pliable and that the horn not in use rolls up and rests against the animal's back. Travelers lucky enough to damage both of the Yale's horns escape with their lives.

Travelers lucky enough to damage both of the Yale's horns escape with their lives

Beasts of both Ethiopia and India are often confused with one another and with other animals. The Yale is no exception. *Ya-el* is the Hebrew word for mountain goat, but the creature is sometimes described as being as large as a hippopotamus. Others interchange the creature with the Catoblepas and the gnu. When one horn is erect, the beast can easily be mistaken for a Unicorn.

The Yale's closest relative is the Centicore, another four-legged beast with two long, straight horns as sharp as spears. This animal, too, lays one horn back when it is fighting. But the horselike Centicore has the chest of a lion, a large round muzzle, and ears that grow in its mouth instead of teeth.

Another relative of the Yale is the flesh-eating Bull of Ethiopia. When it becomes enraged, its horns stand straight up, ready for battle. Its bristly hide is so tough that arrows and spears cannot penetrate it.

The Yale is portrayed in ancient Egyptian paintings, and it guards the temples of India. An African tribe is said to manipulate the horns of its cattle so that one horn points forward like the Yale's. In British heraldry, the Yale is one of the Queen's Beasts and is featured on the arms of Christ's College, Cambridge.

Catoblepas

Poisonous Eyes in a Heavy Head

The deadly Catoblepas (Catoblepe) lives near an Ethiopian spring that is the source of the Nile. Because its head is so heavy that it hangs to the ground, this beast's Greek name means "that which looks downward."

A four-legged creature of moderate size, the Catoblepas has a long mane that falls over its forehead and covers its eyes. Some say this monster is like a bull in appearance; others say it resembles a large boar, with a curling tail and cloven hooves, but that its body is covered with scales. This animal is so lethargic that it would seem to be harmless, but nothing could be further from the truth. Any living creature that meets its venomous eyes falls dead on the spot.

Any living creature that meets its venomous eyes falls dead on the spot

Roman soldiers once came upon a Catoblepas while it was grazing. Thinking it a docile animal fit for food, they approached it with swords drawn. When the beast heard them, it raised its head. Its mane stood up straight and its fatal stare killed them all where they stood. Hearing of this, the captain sent more men to slay the beast, but they, too, died. After the people of the region told the captain of the monster's nature, he commanded his remaining men to surprise it in ambush and to avoid its gaze. In this way was the Catoblepas finally overcome. The soldiers took it to the emperor, who hung its skin in a temple in Rome.

The Catoblepas is also said to have noxious breath, from the poisonous plants on which it feeds. When it is afraid, it curls its lips, opens its mouth wide, and expels a foul air that infects birds, beasts, and humans alike. All lose both sight and voice and are shaken with convulsions that end in death.

This creature has often been confused with the Gorgon and the Basilisk. One early traveler said the Catoblepas lived near the islands of the Gorgon, the monster with snakes instead of hair and with glaring eyes that turn people to stone. Some identify the Catoblepas with the African gnu.

Crocotta

BEAST WITH A HUMAN VOICE

The dog-wolf of India, the Crocotta (Corocotta, Crocuta, Yena), is a deadly enemy of dogs and men. This gluttonous beast digs up the buried dead and prowls about farms at night.

To lure dogs to their death, the Crocotta imitates the sound of a man vomiting. When the dogs hear it, thinking it is a man, they follow the sound, only to be attacked and devoured. The beast sometimes hides in bushes to listen to farmers talking and calling each other by name. The Crocotta then repeats a name, and when the man approaches, it draws back into the brush and speaks the name again. As the man follows, the creature continues to withdraw deeper into the woods. When its unfortunate victim is beyond help from his companions, the animal leaps upon him and feasts upon his flesh.

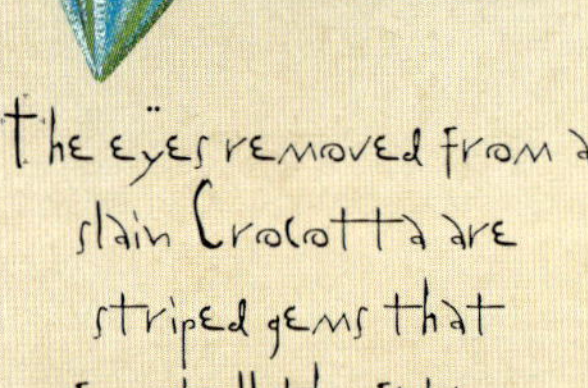

The eyes removed from a slain Crocotta are striped gems that foretell the future

It is said that the Crocotta can change its color at will and that it is alternately male and female. Animals that attempt to circle it stick fast in their own tracks. The eyes removed from a slain Crocotta are striped gems that, when placed under the tongue, foretell the future.

When this creature mates with other animals, its offspring is the Leucrota (Leucrocuta), which also can imitate the sound of the human voice. A cloven-hoofed animal the size of a donkey, the Leucrota is a swift and fierce creature. It has the haunches of a stag, the tail, chest, and neck of a lion, and the head of a badger. Its mouth opens as far back as its ears. Instead of teeth, it has ridges of bone that can crush anything. This animal never closes its eyes, but its backbone is so rigid it is unable to move its head, so it must turn its entire body around to see what is behind it.

The dog-wolf Crocotta and the antelopelike Leucrota are clearly two different kinds of animals, but because of their blood relation, the similarity of their names, and the ability of both to speak with a human voice, naturalists often mistake the one for the other.

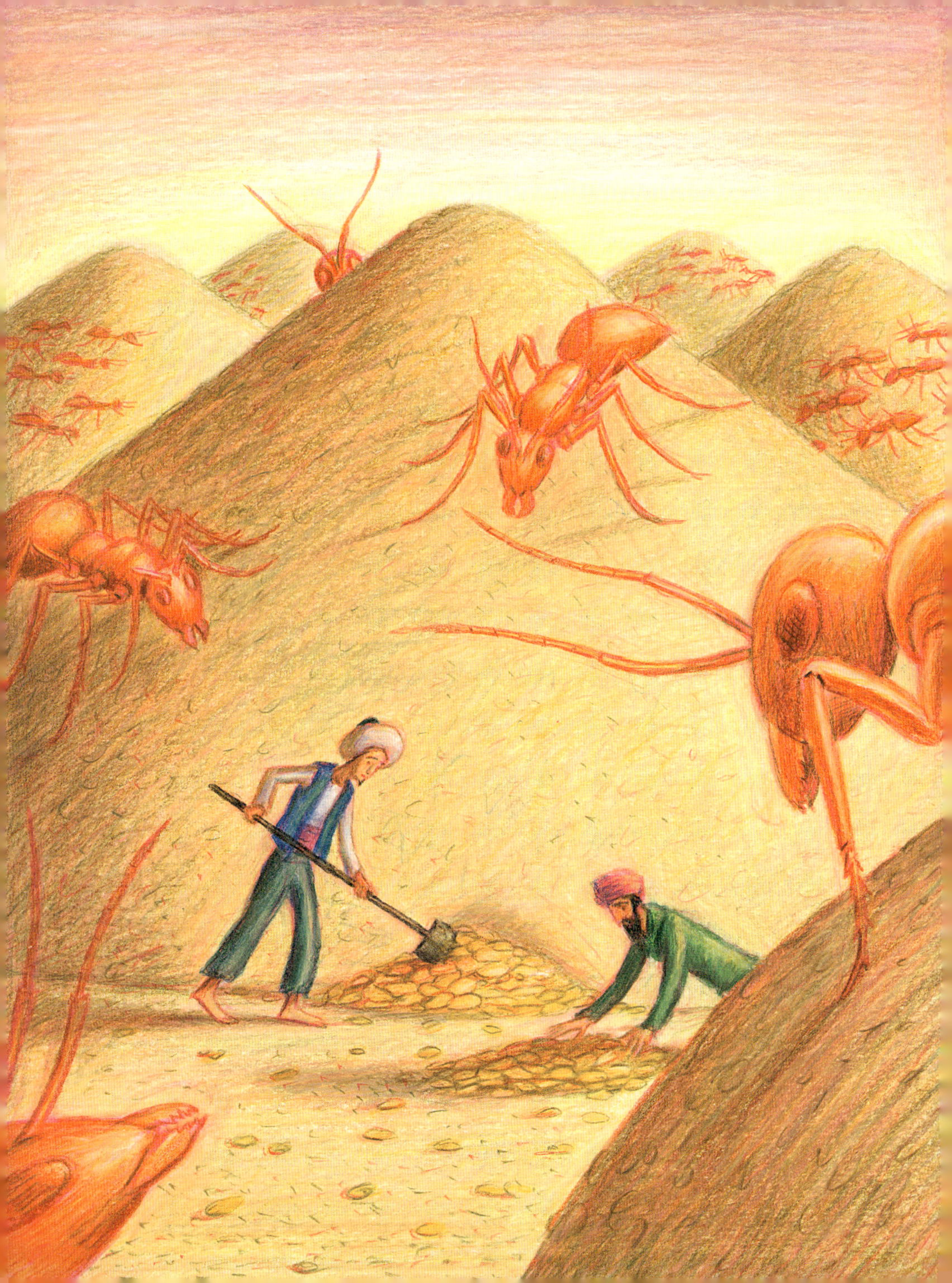

Giant Ants

GUARDIANS OF DESERT GOLD

On a plateau in the remote northern mountains of India, Giant Ants, larger than foxes and some the size of mastiffs, dig gold out of the earth and guard it with their lives. Men who try to steal the gold do so at their peril, for the Giant Ants smell their approach and stream out of their burrows like angry bees. Fierce and swift, they pursue all intruders, and any whom they catch they devour.

The only way to procure the Ants' gold and escape with one's life is to outwit them. The Indians do this by entering their domain in the heat of the day, when the creatures are deep in their burrows. Each of the men rides a female camel with a male camel reined on either side. The treasure seekers approach the burrows stealthily and fill their bags with the gold dust. As they retreat, the enraged Ants emerge from their dens and give chase across the sands. The male camels tire first, collapse, and are eaten by the Ants, but the females gather speed as they rush home to their foals. So reports Herodotus the historian.

The only way to procure the Ants' gold and escape with one's life is to outwit them

Another ploy used to obtain the Ants' treasure is to cut up the flesh of wild beasts and scatter the pieces on the desert sand. When the Ants smell the meat and leave their homes to seek it out, the human intruders hurry to the heaps of sand outside the burrows. They pack the golden prize onto their camels and escape before the Ants return.

Although the Ants are rarely captured, the King of Persia had several of them, brought to him by hunters. Some say the Ants' skins resemble those of leopards. Others refuse to believe that the gold-guarding creatures are indeed ants. They maintain that the beasts are marmots and point out that the Persian word for marmot means mountain ant. Yet others hold that the Giant Ants are really Tibetan miners. Legends telling of enormous ants guarding treasure abound in countries from Greece to China, and an ancient Chinese poet wrote of red ants the size of elephants.

Vegetable Lamb

Is It Plant or Animal?

The Vegetable Lamb of Tartary (Barometz, "little lamb") is one of the rare animals that grows from plants.

From China west to the Caspian Sea, these creatures are born from gourdlike fruit. When the fruit ripens, the husks crack open to reveal little fleecy lambs curled up inside. The growing animals—still attached to their wombs by umbilical cords—venture outside as soon as they are able and feed on surrounding vegetation. Those not devoured by wolves eventually starve after they have consumed all the available food.

An early missionary to China, Friar Odoric, learned of this marvelous animal when he visited the court of the Great Khan. In the Kapsei Mountains, he was told, great gourds grow containing these young lambs. Later travelers have reported eating the tasty flesh of the vegetable beasts.

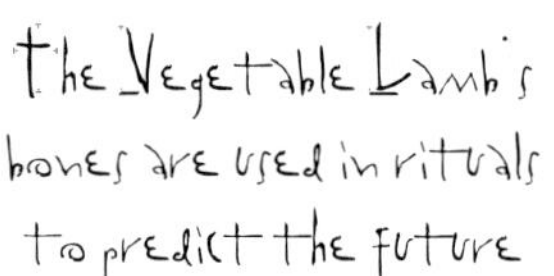

Another kind of Vegetable Lamb is found near the Caspian Sea. From a seed the size of a melon, it grows on a stalk to a height of 2 feet (0.75 meters). It eats all the plants and herbs within its reach. Its hooves are more like compacted hair than solid horn. It is a creature of flesh and blood, and its flesh tastes like crab meat.

The Vegetable Lamb's bones are used in rituals to predict the future. The Tartars prize its soft fleece as material for their caps. The younger the animals are when they are taken, the finer their wool.

The skin of the Vegetable Lamb, too, is highly valued as linings for coats. In England, Queen Elizabeth I's ambassador to Russia obtained such a garment on his journey to the court of the czar. The lambskin coat was later donated to Oxford University, where it was displayed among its collection of rarities.

Not everyone believes the Vegetable Lamb is an actual animal. Detractors point out that the Greek word for fruit means either "melon" or "sheep" and that accounts of the animal arose from a misunderstanding of the word. Some say the creature is a fanciful invention based on the cotton plant.

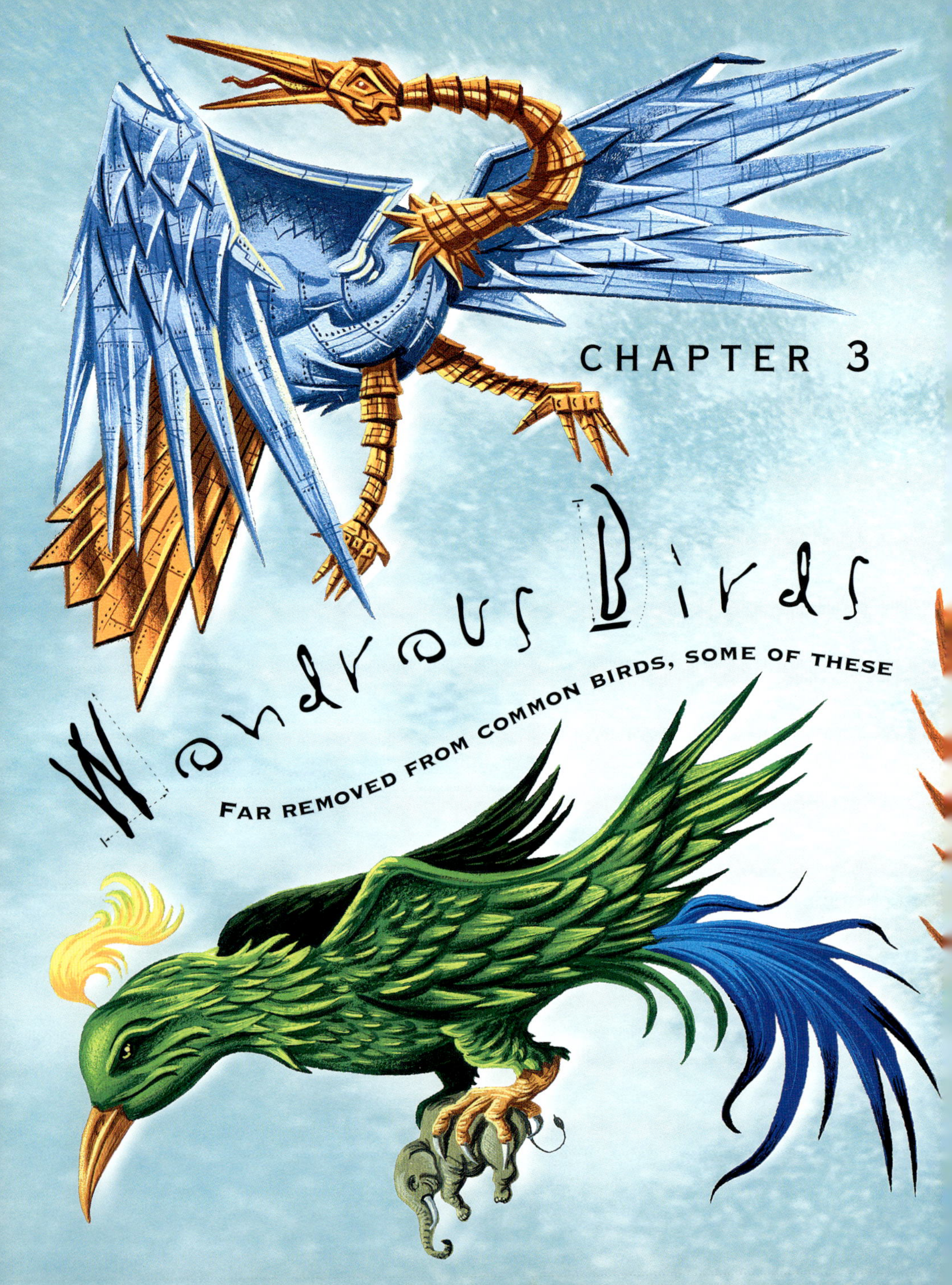

CHAPTER 3

Wondrous Birds

FAR REMOVED FROM COMMON BIRDS, SOME OF THESE

of EARTH & SKY
FABULOUS CREATURES ARE SO LARGE THEY ECLIPSE THE SUN.
OTHERS ARE MAN-EATERS. ONE MAKES THUNDER WITH ITS WINGS.
ONE GLOWS IN THE DARK.
AND THERE ARE MORE.

Bird of the Sun

Born at Creation and worshiped at Heliopolis in ancient Egypt, the Benu (Egyptian hieroglyph, "to shine," "to rise") is a long-legged, heronlike bird with a crest of two long feathers extending from the back of its head. It is an eternal bird that, like the sun, is reborn each morning after its journey through the night. Associated with gods of the sun, it accompanied souls of the dead in the boat of Ra on their voyage through the Underworld.

It accompanied souls of the dead on their voyage through the Underworld

At the beginning of the world, the Benu rose from the primordial sea. The bird was standing on a mound, the earliest land to appear from the dark waters. The first light of the sun shone on the bird and the mound, and when the creature uttered a cry—the breath of life—time began.

Priests of the new human race built a temple on the mound of land that surfaced from the abyss. In this Temple of the Sun, in the city called Heliopolis, they placed a *benben* stone, representing the place the sun-god Atum came in the shape of the Benu bird. The top corners of the *benben's* four sides spread down to a broad base like the rays of the sun. Stones of this shape formed the apex of obelisks erected in rows leading to the temple. The form grew thousands of times over into the great pyramid tombs of the Egyptian pharaohs. In them are pictures of the immortal Benu standing on the *benben* stone at the beginning of all Creation.

The Benu guided souls on their perilous westward journey through the dark Underworld to judgment by the god Osiris. Those that were found worthy sailed on with the bird in the sun-god's boat until they emerged in the East, like the sun, in the light of the afterlife.

When the Greek historian Herodotus visited Egypt, the priests of Heliopolis showed him pictures of the Benu. He called the bird "Phoenix." Many now say that the Western bird that burns to ashes like the setting sun and is reborn in the morning light is a new form of the great Benu of Heliopolis.

Phoenix

Bird That Rises from the Ashes

Many have sought the feather of the eternal Phoenix in order to attain immortality

The eternal Phoenix is a wonder of color. Around its neck is a ruff of gold feathers as bright as the sun, and its wings and long flowing tail feathers are a rainbow of hues. Its beak is like glass, its eyes like jewels, and upon its head is a glowing crest. Even the peacock pales in beauty beside this peerless bird. Only one Phoenix lives in the world at any one time.

Its Greek name means "crimson," "date palm," and "Phoenicia." The date palm ever renews itself, and Phoenicia is "the red land." The Phoenix lives in an earthly paradise far to the East, in the land of Dawn. In its nest high in the tallest tree, the Phoenix rises each morning, greeting the sun with outspread wings and sweet song. Day after day, it bathes in the spring, drinks dew, and lives on air.

Some say the Phoenix lives for 540 years, others 1,461 years, or even more, and many have sought its feather in order to attain immortality. But as the centuries pass, the brilliant plumage fades, and when the bird feels death approaching, it gathers sweet-smelling spices and carries these to a wild desert place, where it builds its pyre in the single date-palm tree. The next morning, when the sunlight strikes the tree, the spices release their oils and the pyre bursts into flame. The bird stands in the fire, fanning the flames with its wings, until it, too, burns and is reduced to ashes.

Then at dusk on the third day, the ashes stir, and from them emerges a worm. Throughout the night, the worm takes on the shape of a bird. Feathers grow, and the next morning a resplendent new Phoenix rises with the sun.

The young bird rolls the ashes into an egg, carries it to Heliopolis, in Egypt, and places the ash-egg on the altar in the Temple of the Sun. Priests record the date of the event before the Phoenix departs for its eastern abode, there to continue its cycle of life, death, and rebirth.

Feng Huang

THE IMMORTAL PHOENIX OF CHINA

Born of the sun and ruling over the southern quadrant, the Chinese Phoenix is emperor of the 360 classes of birds and is one of the four celestial animals.

Feng is the male element of the bird and *huang* the female, the two comprising a yin-and-yang entirety.

The Feng Huang is the most beautiful of all the birds of China. The five colors of its luxuriant plumage—red, azure, yellow, white, and black—represent the cardinal virtues. Its long tail is as bright as fire. Some say it is a composite of other animals, including the swan, unicorn, swallow, snake, fish, crane, drake, dragon, and tortoise. Its song is said to be the source of the Chinese musical scale.

It lives with the single-horned Ki-Lin in the Vermilion Hills, where it nests in the wu-tung tree. The Feng Huang feeds on bamboo shoots and quenches its thirst with dew. Only during a period of peace or when a great sage or benevolent emperor is to be born does the Feng Huang leave the Land of the Immortals and appear in our world as an omen of good fortune. It is joined in its flight by a host of other birds, honoring it as the most magnificent of their kind.

Only during a period of peace does the Feng Huang leave the Land of the Immortals and appear in our world as an omen of good fortune

The first recorded appearance of the Feng Huang was 2647 B.C.E. Pairs of the Chinese Phoenixes built nests in the emperor's garden and charmed lords and ladies with their sweet song. A pair of the immortal birds later gamboled at the court of Emperor Shu during a royal ceremony. And the birds were reported seen many other times.

Sacred to the royal family, the figure of the Feng Huang is embroidered on the robes of empresses and is often paired with the Dragon emblem of the emperor. The Feng Huang and Dragon together are a widespread matrimonial symbol.

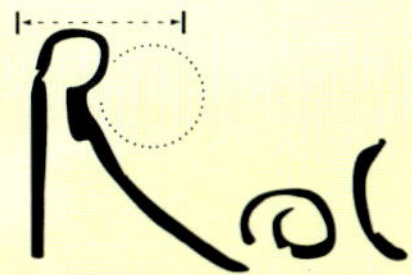

Roc

THE BIRD THAT CARRIES OFF ELEPHANTS

Known as the King of Gigantic Birds, the Roc (Rukh, Ruc) is so vast in size that it darkens the earth with its flight, like a cloud covering the sun. This monster has been sighted from Madagascar to the China Seas. Sailors say it can carry off a ship in its beak.

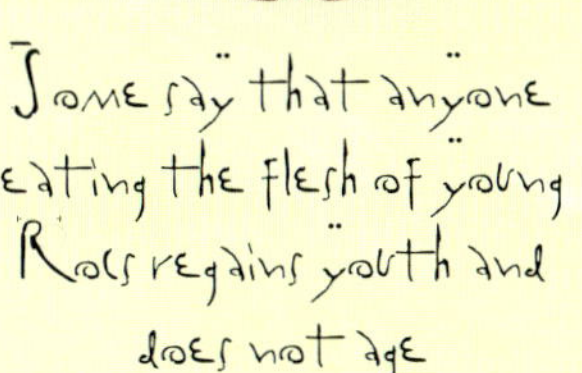

Some say that anyone eating the flesh of young Rocs regains youth and does not age

Sinbad the Sailor encountered a Roc on a remote desert island, where he had been marooned. He escaped from the island by tying himself to the leg of a nesting bird and clinging to a talon as the great creature flew off in search of food. On another voyage, he and his shipmates feasted upon Roc chicks, soon after to be pursued by the parent birds, who dropped boulders on the departing ship. Some say that anyone eating the flesh of young Rocs regains youth and does not age.

Another Arabian traveler, Ibn Batutta, encountered what might have been a Roc in the China Seas. The crew spotted a mountain that was not on any chart, and, when the mountain seemed to rise above the sea, they wept and wailed. The helmsman turned the ship around and a wind carried them away from whatever it was they had seen.

People of the Indian Sea tell of finding a dead Roc whose beak was so large that they cut it off and fashioned it into a ship.

The Rocs of Madagascar prey upon elephants. The birds snatch up the gentle creatures in their claws, lift them into the air, and drop them from great heights. Then they feed on them. These rapacious birds have wingspans of up to thirty paces. Envoys of Kublai Khan bore one of these feathers back to his Chinese court. The emperor was so delighted that he rewarded them with gifts. So says the Venetian traveler Marco Polo.

The Roc's ancestor is the *Aepyornis maxiumus*, the extinct nine-foot-tall (2.7 meters) ostrichlike Elephant Bird of Madagascar. A fossilized egg of the *Aepyornis* has been displayed in the British Museum.

Simurgh

THE WISE OLD BIRD OF AGES

The Simurgh (Senmurv, Saena-Meregha) lives on the peak of Mount Alburz, a sacred Persian mountain that touches the sky. An all-knowing bird with the powers of reason and speech, it once discussed philosophy with King Solomon. Its wings are as broad as clouds and its feathers contain magical restorative powers. Of two natures, both bird and mammal, it suckles its young, like a bat. Some say it lives fifteen hundred years and then revives itself to live fifteen hundred more.

The creature once nested in the Tree of Knowledge. Guarded by thousands of spirits, the tree contained the seeds of all goodness and wisdom. When the Simurgh rose from the tree, a thousand new twigs burst from its shaken branches. And, when the bird lighted in the tree again, a thousand twigs broke off, spreading the seeds of all living things over the earth like rain.

The combination of *si* (thirty) and *murgh* (bird) means thirty birds in one.

Its wings are as broad as clouds and its feathers contain magical restorative powers

Upon finding a Simurgh feather in China, birds of all kinds set out on a pilgrimage to find the great bird. After a long, arduous journey only thirty birds survived. These birds were honored with the revelation that each of them was the Simurgh, and the Simurgh was each and all of them.

When Zal, the white-haired infant son of the warrior Sam, was abandoned on the wooded slope of Mount Alburz, the Simurgh discovered the child and carried him back to its own home above the clouds where it cared for the exiled prince. As the years passed, the Simurgh taught Zal the language of the people and revealed to him the mysteries of the world. One day, Sam rode up the mountain in search of the boy. Telling Zal the two of them must part, the Simurgh offered him a feather telling him if ever he encountered danger he should cast the feather into a fire and the Simurgh would appear. In years to come, both Zal and his son, the hero Rustam, had occasion to invoke the powers of the beneficent bird.

Thunderbird

Power of the Sky

Living among the clouds, the Thunderbird raises the winds when he moves. The air rumbles with the flapping of wings so broad that thunder cracks in different parts of the sky. Arrows of lightning flash from his blinking eyes. And rain pours down to earth from the lake on his back.

He flies across the Americas, changing shape, name, and habits in region after region.

In the Pacific Northwest, he hunts great whales. When a whale rises from a stormy sea, he swoops down upon it, sinks his talons into the hide, and, with the strength of his wings, carries the beast off to a mountaintop. There he feasts upon it, leaving only its bones. Carved likenesses of the Thunderbird and the whale continue to battle on Chilkat totem poles, and one of the tribe appears at gatherings wearing a mask of the great bird and a robe that spreads like wings.

Across the Great Plains and into the eastern woodlands, the Thunderbird is constantly at war with another creature that lives beneath the waters: The Great Horned Watersnake, a monster that lies deep in lakes and ponds and devours anyone entering its territory.

A Comanche hunter of the southern plains once wounded a Thunderbird with an arrow and enlisted his friends to help him kill the creature. But when the braves arrived at the place the bird had fallen, thunder shook the air and lightning flashed, killing one of the men. The others retreated back to their camp.

The Chippeway on the northern shore of Lake Superior say the Thunderbird lives on Thunder Cape. No one climbs to the cliffs to reach its nest because those who tried were killed by the bird's flaming arrows.

Black stones thought to be the arrowheads of the Thunderbird's shafts of lightning can be found across the breadth of the continent. The Thunderbird's recent descendant is the emblematic American eagle, clutching arrows in its talons.

Black stones thought to be the arrowheads of the Thunderbird's shafts of lightning can be found across the breadth of the continent

Perÿton

Deer with an Avian Body

The Peryton has the antlered head and legs of a deer and the wings and body of a bird. A mortal enemy of humans, it casts the shadow of a man until it kills one, at which time its shadow becomes that of itself. It can kill only one man in its lifetime.

Perytons lived in Atlantis until an earthquake shattered that mysterious civilization and all traces of it sank to the bottom of the sea. All traces, that is, except for the Perytons who escaped into the air during the disaster and were later sighted flying in great flocks high above the Pillars of Hercules.

A Sibyl once prophesied that Perytons would bring about the downfall of Rome. While scholars attribute the decline of the classical world to causes other than Perytons, the monsters are said to have tried to disrupt the course of the empire.

A mortal enemy of humans. it casts the shadow of a man until it kills one

It was during the time that Hannibal and his armies were massed outside the walls of Rome, waiting for more support before making a final attack. Meanwhile, a young Roman general named Scipio had received permission from the emperor to transport his legions across the Mediterranean to Africa.

The Roman fleet had been at sea only days when the first Peryton descended from the sky. Its shadow on the deck was that of a man, but, after it gored an oarsman to death, the shadow changed to the beast's antlered form. Other Perytons followed, hundreds of the monsters swooping down upon the ships. Many shadows changed from men to Perytons before Scipio relayed the order for his soldiers to raise their shields toward the sun and blind the beasts. The surviving Perytons flew away and the next day the Romans sighted the coast of Africa.

As winged creatures that are mortal enemies of humans, Perytons are distantly related to the Stymphalids.

Stymphalids

BRAZEN ARCHERS OF THE MARSHES

Stymphalids are man-eating birds with brass beaks and claws that can pierce armor

Similar to cranes in size and shape, Stymphalids are man-eating birds with brass beaks and claws that can pierce armor. Their feathers, too, are brass, which they shoot from their wings like arrows.

These birds are named for the shadowy marshes of Stymphalus, in Arcadia, where they once lived. They were dreaded creatures that terrorized neighboring farms and villages, killing men and animals and poisoning fields with their excrement. Ridding the marsh of the monsters was one of the Twelve Labors of Hercules. The Greek hero had already killed the Hydra of Lerna and other beasts. Destroying the Stymphalids, too, was no easy task. The thousands of beasts that clattered over the waters and nested in reeds and rocky cliffs far outnumbered his arrows. The goddess Athena came to his aid, giving him a pair of bronze rattles. He climbed to the highest point above the marsh and shook the rattles with all his might. The clanging shattered the air, sending the entire flock screeching up into the sky in terror. Hercules shot as many of the birds as he had arrows, and the others flew away, never to return.

Some of the Stymphalids fled to the island of the war god Ares, where Jason and his crew encountered them on their voyage in quest of the Golden Fleece. The men knew that Hercules had frightened the birds with the din of the goddess's rattles. When their ship approached the island, the warriors terrified the birds by banging on their bronze shields with their swords. The men then covered themselves with the bucklers as the panicked birds flew overhead, sending volleys of their brass arrows ringing against the roof of shields. Jason and his crew sailed away unharmed.

The other Stymphalids routed by Hercules flew on to the desert of Arabia, where they still live today.

Figures of the birds are carved on a temple in Stymphalus, reminders of the days long gone, when the birds tyrannized the countryside.

Siren

ALLURING SINGER

Sirens (Greek, "to bind," "to draw with a rope") are beguiling creatures whose sweet song promises the wisdom of the ages and the fulfillment of all desires. On the rocky Siren Isles, off the southern coast of Italy, they play lyres to accompany their singing. But listeners who succumb to their enchantment never return home. Mariners whom the music lulls to sleep are torn to pieces. Those who leap into the sea to join the singers drown in the waves.

Early Sirens, daughters of a Muse, were birds with golden plumage and the faces of young girls. Others had birds' feet and feathered lower bodies and the forms of women from the waist up. Some of these once challenged the Muses themselves to a singing contest, but the Muses won and plucked out the Sirens' feathers to wear as crowns. The shamed bird-women retreated to the desert islands now named after them.

Jason and his Argonauts approached these rocks on their homeward voyage with the Golden Fleece. Perched above the harbor, among bones covered with scraps of flesh, the Sirens greeted the ship with their seductive melodies. The oarsmen stopped rowing to listen. Before they could be enthralled, another of the crew, Orpheus, began to play the lyre that charmed all nature. His song filled the ears of his companions and a wind carried the ship on. The despondent Sirens dropped into the sea, becoming rocks along the shore.

The hero Ulysses also sailed near the Siren Isles, but the witch Circe had warned him of the danger. Wanting to hear the Sirens' song, he stopped the ears of his men with beeswax and had them tie him to the mast. As his crew bent to the oars, he listened to the sweet but deadly singers. "Come to us for knowledge of all that will happen on the bountiful earth," they sang. Ulysses begged his men to loosen the ropes that bound him, but they rowed on, leaving the Sirens behind them.

Listeners who succumb to
their enchantment
never return home

Since the Middle Ages, Sirens have had the tails of fish and feet of falcons. They are closely related to Mermaids.

Cinnamon Bird

Source of Arabian Spices

Among the sweet spices of Arabia is cinnamon, once more precious than gold. Although its place of origin is unknown, this rare spice is brought to Arabia by the Cinnamon Bird (Cynomolgus), which uses it as material for its nest. One can gather the cinnamon in two different ways, depending on where the birds build their homes.

One can gather the cinnamon in two different ways depending on where the birds build their homes

The larger variety of Cinnamon Bird attaches its sticks with mud to the sheer face of cliffs. Unable to climb the smooth rock, gatherers have devised their own method of acquiring the cinnamon. They bring with them pieces of flesh they have cut from dead beasts of burden. After scattering the meat beneath the nests, the men draw back far enough away from the site so the birds will not be disturbed. The Cinnamon Birds fly down, grasp the meat in their claws, and carry it up to their nests. When the nests will no longer hold the weight of the carrion, they pull away from the rock and break apart on the ground. The Arabians then rush in, collect the cinnamon sticks, and carry off their prize, which they sell to traders from other countries.

A smaller kind of Cinnamon Bird builds its nest of spices in the top of the tallest palm tree it can find. The men attach leaden tips to arrows and shoot them up into the nests until the weight of the lead dislodges the cinnamon from the tree. The Arabians then gather up the spices and sell them to the highest bidder. Bestiaries picture men slinging weighted missiles at the nest.

Every spice of Arabia is acquired by a different method. To obtain frankincense, Arabians must burn a gum whose smoke drives away the winged serpents that guard the spice-bearing trees. Aromatic labdanum is more easily extracted from the beards of goats.

The Cinnamon Bird is closely related to the Phoenix, which builds its nest of cinnamon, frankincense, cassia, and other sweet-smelling spices of Arabia.

Barnacle Goose

A Wonder of Nature

Regarded as a fish or a fruit. roasted Barnacle Goose has been enjoyed during periods of fasting

The Barnacle Goose (Tree Goose) is born not from other geese but from water-soaked wood or fruit-bearing trees. Because it does not breed or lay eggs, no nest of this marvel has ever been found, but the bird has been observed, in all stages of growth, from the coasts of the Irish Sea up to the Orkney Islands about twenty miles off the northeast coast of Scotland. The adult bird has black feet, a black bill, and black and white feathers. Regarded as a fish or a fruit, roasted Barnacle Goose has been enjoyed during periods of fasting.

On a windswept island off Lancashire, England, the beach is strewn with the ribs of wrecked ships and the branches of broken trees. From this rotted wood, thousands of mussel-like shells hang from filmy stems. In some shells, balls of soft down breathe, nourished by seawater and wood sap. Tiny webbed feet dangle from gaping shells, while from other shells fully formed goslings hang by their black bills. After dropping to the shore, the young birds scurry into the water. Once they are full-fledged, they are larger than a mallard but smaller than a goose. This is the way the Barnacle Goose is born from barnacles.

Farther up the coast, growing at the water's edge, are trees that bear gourdlike fruit. When the husks split open, the fruit is revealed as Tree Geese, hanging by their beaks. The goslings that drop onto the land die. Those that drop into the sea swim away.

The Barnacle Goose has been the subject of learned controversy ever since the 1200s. Pope Innocent III, concluding that the bird was born of mortal flesh, prohibited the eating of Barnacle Goose during Lent. Despite eyewitness accounts of authors who have seen the bird emerge from shells, many authorities maintain that barnacles are marine crustaceans and Barnacle Geese are actual birds (classified as *Anser bernicla*), hatched from eggs.

The Tree Goose variety of the Barnacle Goose is related to the Vegetable Lamb of Tartary, another animal born from a plant.

Caladrius

HEALER IN THE HALLS OF KINGS

The Caladrius (Charadrius) is highly prized because of its diagnosis of the sick and its curative powers. In the presence of an ill person, this bird will indicate whether the patient will live or die. If the person can be cured, the creature will even speed his or her recovery. The bird's cure is especially effective for jaundice, and the flesh of its inner thigh can cure blindness.

In the presence of an ill person this bird will indicate whether the patient will live or die

The Caladrius is white, with no black at all. It has the graceful neck of a swan and yellow beak and legs. Originally from Persia, the bird can now be found in royal palaces in many countries. Rulers have sought the bird ever since Alexander the Great discovered its diagnostic powers. When it is placed before an ill person, it first determines whether he or she is capable of cure. If the sickness is trapped within the patient and death is certain, the bird turns its head away. But, if the disease is not fatal, the bird faces the patient and absorbs the noxious vapors of the illness. As the patient's complexion returns to normal, the bird's pure-white plumage turns to gray. With the sickness now inside itself, it flies out into the open, toward the sun, dispelling the poison into the air. Its feathers return to white.

The Caladrius is not popular among court doctors, who are frequently proved wrong by the bird's diagnosis and cures. The bird's powers are also troublesome to the sellers of birds, because people who are ill will visit a shop with no intention of actually purchasing a Caladrius. They will simply approach the bird and look it in the eye to learn its diagnosis. If the bird can cure them on the spot, it will, ingesting the sickness into itself and flying out of the shop. Even though the bird returns to its owner, the shopkeeper has lost a potential sale—regardless of whether the customer has been cured or is sure to die. Most bird sellers now keep their Caladrius in a back room until they are certain a customer is serious about purchasing the bird.

Bird of Paradise

Spirit of Rare Beauty

The Bird of Paradise (Manucodiata, "Birds of God") is a vision of iridescent color. Its long flowing plumage, as light as gossamer, shines golden, orange, emerald green, and chestnut brown. Without flesh or bone, this bright spirit lives in Paradise, where it feeds on dew. It descends to earth only to rest. Lacking feet, it attaches itself to the branch of a tree with two strings that extend beyond its tail feathers.

No one has ever seen a living Bird of Paradise, nor has anyone ever discovered its nest or eggs. Naturalists speculate that the female bird lays its eggs in a depression on the male's back and that they hatch while the bird remains in flight. Only after a Bird of Paradise dies and its body is discovered on earth are human beings able to look upon its beauty.

Only after a Bird of Paradise dies and its body is discovered on earth are human beings able to look upon its beauty

People of the East Indies were the first to discover the bodies of these birds, radiant with color and light as air. Rulers wore the feathers in battle, believing them to be as strong as armor. Knowing the live birds never touch the ground, hunters cover strings and reeds with lime and hang them in the air, but the entangled birds die in the trap.

It was two birds such as these that the Sultan of Batjan, in the Moluccas, presented to the captain of the *Victoria* as a gift to the King of Spain. Having completed the first circumnavigation of the world, the *Victoria* returned to Spain with a full cargo of cloves and two dead birds. Some said the footless birds later traded to Europe were fakes prepared and dried by natives. The feathers of these birds were in great demand as decoration for women's hats. Two live birds called Birds of Paradise were given to the London Zoo during the reign of Queen Victoria. It was said they were the first of their kind to be seen alive in Europe.

Aristotle said there could be no such creature as a footless bird, but the scientific name of the Bird of Paradise is *Paradisea apoda*, meaning "without feet."

Cucuio

Light in the Darkness

When several of the creatures are joined together they can be substituted for candles or torches

The Cucuio (Cocuie) of the West Indies is one of those rare birds that gives off its own light. No larger than a thumb, it has four wings, and eyes that shine as bright as lamps.

People capture them to use as a source of light. When several of the creatures are joined together, they can be substituted for candles or torches. Men and women of the Indies carry them in the dark to light their way. Bookkeepers and seamstresses can work late at night in the glow of their eyes. Armies on the march prefer them to torches because the light of the Cucuio cannot be extinguished by wind or rain.

When the birds' eyes begin to dim with use, people release the animals until the glow returns, at which time they are caught once again. The Cucuio also has eyes under its wings, but these are bright only when the bird flies free. After a bird dies, people have been known to squeeze the luminescence out of its body and spread it on their faces, making them glow in the darkness.

A close relative of the Cucuio is the Ercinee, which is born in the Hercynian Forest of Germany. This bird lights its own way through the darkest night with the glow of its feathers. A phosphorescence that falls from its wings marks its progress.

Some say both the Cucuio and the Ercinee are actually fireflies, not birds at all. However, there is no question about their light-producing cousin, the Alicanto. This bird seeks its food from mineral veins in the Chilean mountains. When it eats gold, it shines like the sun. When it gorges on silver, it glows like the moon. Travelers who have heard of this bird will follow a light that weaves through the darkness, hoping the light is the Alicanto and that it will lead them to riches.

The people of the Indies, the Hercynian Forest of Germany, and the mountains of Chile all say that one should take care in following the lights of these birds, because they may dim at any time, leaving one lost in the wilderness at night.

CHAPTER 4

Fantastic Fish of the SEA

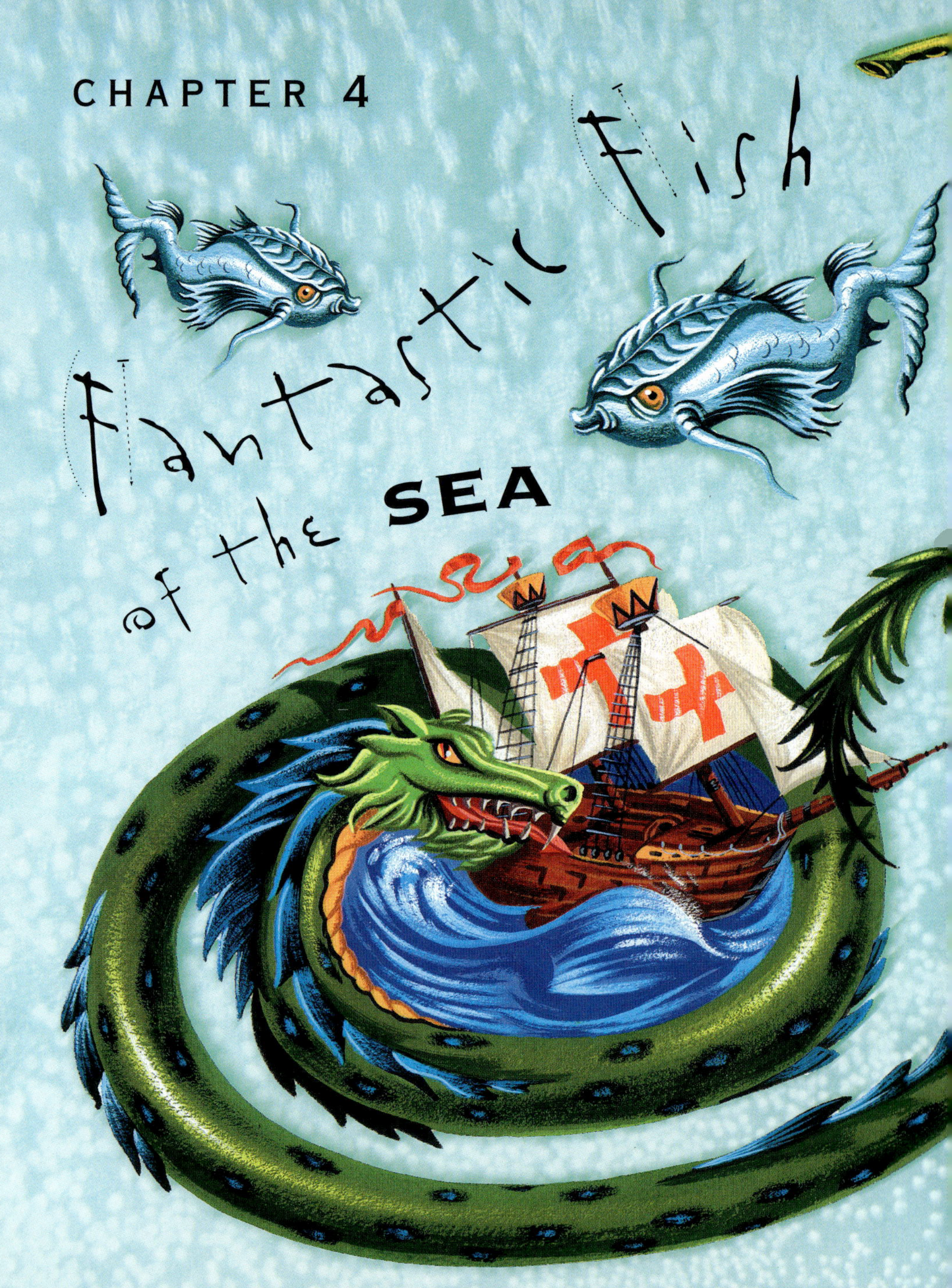

Fabled creatures of the deep are as large as islands and as small as a human hand.

Some sink ships and swallow crews.

Some with sweet voices lure sailors to their doom.

Others pull the chariots of sea-kings.

Aspidochelone

The Island Beast

The Aspidochelone (Asp Turtle or Shield Turtle) is the largest and most deceptive monster that lives in the sea. Its hide is so thick and rough that it looks like a rocky shore, and the creature is so large that, when it is sleeping on the surface of the water, one can easily mistake it for an island. This sea beast is known by many names, including Jasconius ("fish"), Cetus ("whale"), Leviathan, and the Island Beast. Some say one of its kind swallowed Jonah.

When Alexander the Great was in India, people on shore pointed to an island in the middle of the sea. They said an ancient king was buried there with much treasure. Not wanting Alexander to risk the danger, his closest friend took a boatload of men to the island. They disembarked and, within the hour, the island sank, drowning all who ventured onto it. Days later, Alexander saw the tusked beast they all had thought was solid land.

The creature is so large that when it is sleeping on the surface of the water one can easily mistake it for an island

On Sinbad the Sailor's first voyage, the captain anchored on a sandy island dotted with palm trees. The crew prepared the cooking fires. While some ate and drank, and others bathed in tubs, Sinbad wandered off to explore. The island shook beneath them, sending sailors scurrying back to the ship. Before Sinbad could reach safety, the monster dived, carrying him and others down with it. Sinbad crawled into a floating tub and drifted through the night to a real island.

The Irish St. Brendan and his crew of monks were sailing in their *curragh* (a boat made of animal hides) to the Promised Land of the Saints when they, too, came upon the beast. They celebrated mass on the creature and built fires to boil and salt raw meat. When the island began to move, the monks rushed back to their boat and the creature swam out to sea. The fires on its back could be seen for two miles.

Sea Serpent

Monster of the Deep

One of the most feared creatures in the ocean, the Sea Serpent has been known to coil itself around ships and swallow entire crews.

> Sea Serpents are easy to recognize: they swim with their long necks extended upward and their horselike heads covered with manes resembling seaweed

Hundreds of reported sightings of beasts of this kind indicate that they are between 60 and 300 feet (18 and 90 meters) long. Their scaly backs are dark gray or brown and their underbellies white. Sea Serpents are easy to recognize: They swim with their long necks extended upward, their horselike heads covered with manes resembling seaweed. Behind them, their humps rise above the surface of the water like a string of floating casks.

The Great Norway Serpent is said to be more than 200 feet (61 meters) long and 20 feet (6 meters) thick. It is black and scaly. Long hair hangs from its head. It lives in caves along the coast, and on summer nights it ventures inland to feed on lambs and calves. Out on the sea, it terrifies sailors when its neck rises from the water as high as their mast and the beast's great head sweeps down to devour the unfortunate. These occurrences always portend dire events in the kingdom, such as war or the downfall of a ruler.

Whalers of the northern seas have watched a Sea Serpent, with head raised, glide silently into a pod of unsuspecting sperm whales. The sea beast coils itself around a whale and crushes it to death.

Off the North American coast, at Gloucester Harbor, Massachusetts, fishermen reported seeing a sea snake about 70 feet (21 meters) long, its head lifted high above the water. Their story was dismissed as fanciful until a crowd numbering hundreds gathered on the shore and saw the creature with their own eyes. Sailors armed with rifles set out in boats to kill the beast, but it disappeared beneath the waves.

The Sea Serpent best known today is the monster reported seen in the misty waters of Scotland's Loch Ness.

Sea Beast with Many Arms

Of all the monsters of the northern ocean, the Kraken is one of the most feared. It sleeps at the bottom of the sea. When it rises to the surface, its back spreads to a mile and a half (2.5 kilometers) in circumference, looking at first like an island. The waving tentacles that follow stretch as tall as a ship's mast. It wraps these arms around unwary ships and plucks sailors from the decks. Then it sinks back into the deep, pulling the waters after it into a giant whirlpool. The greatest of these vortexes is the Maelstrom off the coast of Norway, which has sucked many a ship into a watery grave.

Fishermen say one of its eyes would fill a small boat and the pupil of the eye is so fiery that at night it looks like a bonfire burning in the sea

Olaus Magnus's map of the northern seas portrays this "midnight wonder" as a beast with long tentacles like a tree pulled up by its roots. Fishermen say one of its eyes would fill a small boat, and the pupil of the eye is so fiery that, at night, it looks like a bonfire burning in the sea.

A smaller relative of the Kraken was captured in ancient times off the coast of Spain. In the dark of night, it would come ashore from the open sea and raid the inland fish pools. Even fences could not keep the monster out, and it took men with three-pronged harpoons to kill the beast. Its head was as big as a 90-gallon (340-liter) barrel, and its arms were 30 feet (9 meters) long. Weighing 700 pounds (320 kilograms), the specimen was put on public display as a curiosity.

Carcasses of many like this have washed ashore on northern beaches, and a French warship, the *Alecton*, came upon such a beast, floating on the surface of the water. Mistaking it at first for the wreckage of a vessel, the crew discovered that it was a living monster. Harpoons sank into it harmlessly, and, at first, even cannonballs failed to dispatch it. At last a ball hit a vital spot, and the creature's body sank beneath the waves.

Popularly known as the giant squid, the Kraken's modern kind has seldom been seen since the crew of the *Alecton* told their tale to a disbelieving public.

Bishop Fish

Churchman of the Ocean

Everything on the earth and in the sky has its counterpart in the depths of the sea. There are mountains and forests, flowers and vines, and fishes that mirror all that is in the air and on the land. There are starfish and sunfish, swordfish and sawfish, cucumber fish, catfish, dogfish, sea lions, sea elephants, seahorses, sea cows, and sea swine. There are even Mermaids and Mermen, and among these are fishes in the shape of bishops.

Sailors are reminded of church when they spot the creature known as the Bishop Fish

The Bishop of the Sea appears to wear a miter on its head and vestments on its shoulders. Its body is covered with scales. Sailors are reminded of church when they spot this creature. A Bishop Fish was caught in 1531 and taken to the king of Poland. The king wished to keep it at the palace to display to his subjects, but the creature gestured to the clergy in the court that it wished to return to the sea. They granted its request. It is said that, at the shore, it gave the sign of the cross before disappearing into the waves. Some unbelievers said the Sea Bishop was no bishop at all, but was in fact a walrus.

A related cleric of the waters, sometimes seen accompanying the Bishop Fish, is the Monk Fish, with a shaved head and wearing the habit of a cleric. This creature was reportedly taken by sailors in a stormy sea off the coast of Norway. These maritime holy men are described in the books of fishes of Conrad Gesner and others. The Sea Monk of China also has a shaved head and scaly body. It is a fierce creature that capsizes junks.

The Bishop Fish and Monk Fish are modern descendants of the classical Triton and the Mermen of ancient Mesopotamia. The Triton was so heavy that, when it climbed onto a ship at night and sat on its side, the vessel would tip and take in water. A Triton displayed in Rome had the nose, ears, mouth, and hands of a man, but its body was rough and scaly, and it had a tail instead of feet.

Mermaid

The Deadly Face of Beauty

Half human and half fish, the maiden of the sea has the head and torso of a beautiful woman and the lower body of a fish with fluked tail. This alluring creature with blue-green eyes sits upon a rock in the sea. Holding a mirror in one hand, she tends her long hair with a golden comb. She uses the comb to pluck her lyre and enchant mariners with the sweetness of her song.

Heartless and vain. she brings misfortune to all who see her

But there is a dark side to the beauty of the Mermaid. Heartless and vain, she brings misfortune to all who see her. Ships and crews have been lost at sea after sailors saw her lounging on a rock or frolicking among the waves in stormy weather. She and her kind live in dangerous waters off the coasts of northern seas. They can assume human shape when they visit land.

Many sailors have fallen in love with Mermaids and have followed the seductive creatures into the sea, never to be seen again. After lulling crews to sleep with their sweet voices, some Mermaids have boarded ships and carried off sailors. Some have killed those who refused to lie with them—and even eaten their flesh.

Captain Richard Whitbourne reported standing in a harbor in Newfoundland when he saw a sea creature with long blue hair and the face of a woman swimming toward him. When he stepped back in surprise, the Mermaid dived and disappeared. Members of the crew said the creature later approached their small boat. When it grasped the side and tried to climb aboard, the frightened sailors hit it with their oars and it swam away.

On Henry Hudson's second voyage in search of the Northwest Passage to the East Indies, one of the crew called out that a Mermaid was swimming beside the ship. Others joined him to see a Mermaid with long black hair. When a wave turned her over, they saw that her skin was white and her breasts were like a woman's. Then she dived, flashing a tail that was speckled like a mackerel.

Some say Mermaids are common sea creatures like dugongs and manatees.

Hippocampus

WATER HORSE

The Hippocampus (Greek for "horse" and "sea monster"; Sea Horse) is one of the many sea creatures resembling animals on land. The most common Sea Horse has the head and forelegs of a horse, the scaly lower body of a fish, and the fluked tail of a dolphin. Others of its kind have webbed paws instead of hooves and a fin for a mane. Some have wings like Pegasus, or even the horn of a Unicorn. All of these live in the great oceans of the world.

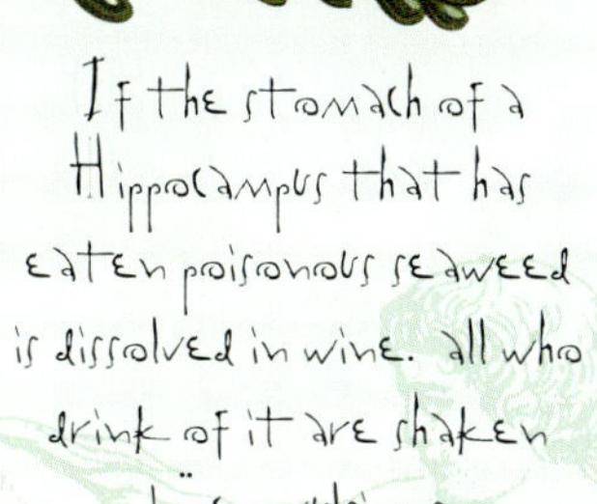

Ancient ancestors of the Hippocampus pulled the chariot of the sea god Poseidon (Neptune), and his Nereid daughters rode upon their backs. When the god struck the water with his trident, raising the winds, these horses of the sea looked like foaming waves galloping to the shore.

If the stomach of a Hippocampus that has eaten poisonous seaweed is dissolved in wine, all who drink of it are shaken by convulsions. Those who survive lose their memories and sink into insanity. Craving to be near water, they journey to the sea in which the creature once lived and wade along the shore.

Hippocampus is a genus of small fishes with heads shaped like those of a horse and scaly bodies that end in curling tails. This name also applies to parts of the human brain that resemble those fish. The Sea Horse is a heraldic beast and swims in the seas of old maps.

Others in the vast family of marine animals also share a name with their counterparts on solid land. The Sea Lion, with the head of a lion, webbed forefeet, and the tail of a fish, roars like the King of Beasts. The Sea Swine, which bears a half-moon on its back and eyes on its scaly sides, tastes like pork. The Sea Monkey has an apelike face, but its body is covered with a shell like that of a tortoise. The Sea Hare is a mollusk with the coloring, head, and feet of a rabbit.

Little Wonder of the Sea

Only 6 inches (15 centimeters) long, this little fish changed the fate of Rome and human history. Named Remora by the Romans because it is a "delay," or "hindrance," and Echeneis by the Greeks, because it is a "ship-holder," this gray-colored creature is just the length of a hand. With a sucker disk on the top of its head, the Remora attaches itself to a ship under full sail and, by a power far greater than its size, abruptly stops the progress of the vessel, as surely as an anchor or a cable. The historian Pliny the Elder called the fish the grandest of nature's wonders.

The forces of Octavian, the leader of the western Roman Empire, and Mark Antony, the master of the eastern sector, engaged at Actium in a sea battle that would determine the course of Rome. Antony commanded the fleet of Cleopatra, Queen of Egypt. Their five hundred large warships far surpassed the Roman fleet in numbers and size. At the height of the battle, a tiny Remora attached itself to the hull of Antony's flagship, stopping the vessel in the water.

When worn as an amulet by pregnant women the Remora is said to prevent miscarriages

In the confusion that followed, the ships in the center and left of the phalanx returned to the harbor and Antony retreated to the galley of Cleopatra. The lovers sailed for Egypt, leaving victory to Rome and to Octavian, who was to become the emperor Caesar Augustus.

A later Roman emperor, Caligula, did not fare as well after his encounter with the Remora. His fleet was in full sail when one ship, the emperor's quinquereme, manned by four hundred oarsmen, slowed and stopped. Men who dived off the ship to discover what had halted its progress found a little Remora attached to the rudder. When they brought the fish on board, it had no more power than a slug. Caligula was furious that such a tiny creature had detained the voyage of a divine emperor. The delay boded ill for Caligula, for after returning to Rome he was assassinated.

When worn as an amulet by pregnant women, the Remora is said to prevent miscarriages, delaying birth.

Micropedia

MORE BEASTS FROM MYTHOLOGY, CLASSICAL WRITINGS, BESTIARIES, AND FOLKLORE AROUND THE WORLD

AITVARAS: A Lithuanian rooster with four dragon legs and a fiery tail. It brings farmers gifts of coins and grain in exchange for omelettes.

AMPHIPTERE: A timid winged serpent with large eyes. It has been known to flee at the approach of villagers.

ANKA: A gigantic Arabian bird that lives 1,700 years. Its wingspan is the breadth of five elephants side by side.

ANT-LION: A little beast that cannot eat plants because of its lion father, nor can it live on meat because of its ant mother, so it starves to death.

BONNACON: A bovine creature that eludes hunters by emitting excrement that sets fire to trees and bushes.

CAMELOPARD: The spotted offspring of a camel and a leopard. It is sometimes called a giraffe.

CERBERUS: A three-headed dog that guards the entrance to the Underworld. It is offered honeycakes in return for the safe passage of souls of the dead.

FIREBIRD: A magical Russian bird with jeweled eyes and flaming feathers. It steals golden apples from royal gardens.

HARPY (GREEK, "SNATCHER"): A ravenous monster with the face of an old crone, the body of a vulture, long curved claws, and filthy underparts.

HALULU: Man-eating Hawaiian birds whose feathers are made of water from the sun. Halulu can assume human form.

HERCYNIAN STAG: An ox-shaped stag from whose forehead grows a single horn that spreads out like palm leaves. It lives in the Hercynian Forest of Germany.

HIPPOGRIFF: A winged creature with the foreparts of an eagle-Griffin and the hindparts of a horse. It once carried a knight around the world.

ILERION (ALLERION): Only two of these birds of India are alive at any one time. When their two chicks are hatched, the parent birds drown themselves.

MO-O (MO-KO): A great sea Dragon of Polynesia. The people of the islands say it once moved an oyster bed from their shores to another part of the ocean.

NESS MONSTER: A man-eating water beast in the River Ness, once driven off by St. Columba. An ancestor of "Nessie," the Loch Ness Monster.

ODONTOTYRANNOS (GREEK, "TOOTH-KING"): A gigantic one-horned monster that attacked the camp of Alexander the Great. It took 1,300 men to drag away the slain beast.

PARANDRUS: An Ethiopian beast with branching horns and a shaggy coat the color of a bear. When hunted, it changes color to blend in with its surroundings.

PELUDA: Said to have survived the Great Flood, the French Peluda has a serpent head and tail, a body with shaggy green fur, and tortoiselike feet.

QUESTING BEAST: King Arthur once observed this beast with a serpent's head and leonine body. It made a sound like hounds baying in its stomach.

QUETZALCOATL (AZTEC; MAYAN, "KUKULKAN"): The Plumed Serpent of Mexico and Central America—a snake with the feathers of the quetzal bird.

SCYLLA: Once a beautiful nymph, Scylla was transformed into a monster with twelve feet, six long necks, and three rows of teeth in each head.

SERRA: A flying fish that races ships, but always tires and dives back into the sea. It sometimes spreads its wings downwind of sails to stop ships' progress.

SHANG YANG: A one-legged Chinese bird that drinks the sea dry and blows the water out again like rain. It can change its own height.

SLEIPNIR: Swift eight-legged horse that carried the Norse god Odin through the sky, over land, and down into the Underworld.

STRANGE SEA CREATURE: As pictured in old natural histories, this monster is round like a tortoise, with four eyes and ears, and twelve legs.

TENGU: Mischievous Japanese bird-men with long hooked beaks and feathered wings. Some wear cloaks and black hats. They live in palaces on mountaintops.

THREE-LEGGED ASS: A Persian beast as large as a mountain. It has nine mouths, six eyes, and a single hollow horn of gold.

TI-CHIANG: A bright-red Chinese bird with four wings and six feet, but no face or eyes. It lives in the Mountains of the Sky.

ZIPHIUS: A water owl with a wedge-shaped beak and cavernous mouth. As large as a whale, it attacks any ship that sails near it.

ZIZ: A Hebrew bird so big that when it stands in the middle of an ocean the water comes up only to its knees.

Reading List

Medieval bestiarists seldom attributed their sources. Nearly all the primary sources listed below are among the sources for the later bestiaries or for natural histories through the Renaissance. I derived most of the material in *The Book of Dragons and Other Mythical Beasts* from these works. This annotated list is chronological. A bibliography of my major secondary sources follows on the facing page.

Primary Sources

Ancient: *Enuma Elish*, the Babylonian Epic of Creation (Tiamat and Marduk) • The Egyptian *Book of the Dead* (the Benu)
Classical: Homer, *The Odyssey* (Ulysses and the Sirens) • *Hymn to Apollo*, from *The Homeric Hymns* (Apollo and Python) • Hesiod, *Theogony* (Echidna and the birth of monsters) • Herodotus, *The History* (the first major descriptions of the Phoenix, Giant Ants, Cinnamon Bird, and Griffin) • Ctesias, *Indica* (the first major descriptions of the Manticore, Unicorn, and Crocotta) • Aristotle, *Historia Animalium* (the Cinnamon Bird) • Apollodorus, *The Library* (classical myths) • Ovid, *The Metamorphoses* (the Phoenix; Perseus, Andromeda, and Cetus) • Pomponius Mela, *The Situation of the World* (a source for Pliny the Elder; the Catoblepas and the Dragons of India) • Pliny the Elder, *Natural History* (Pliny's beasts of Ethiopia passage, one of the most famous in all fabulous-animal literature; the Leucrota, Yale, Manticore, Unicorn, Catoblepas, and Basilisk) • Lucan, *Pharsalia* (the standard source of bestiary serpents; the Amphisbaena, Jaculus, Scytale, Seps, and Dipsa) • Pausanias, *Description of Greece* (the Stymphalids) • Aelian, *On Animals* (a major bestiary source) • Philostratus, *The Life of Apollonius of Tyana* (animal marvels of India) • Solinus, *Collection of Remarkable Facts* (a major bestiary source, echoing Pliny; Draconce) • Lactantius, *Phoenix* (the first extensive telling of the Phoenix fable)
Medieval: *Physiologus* (ancestor of the bestiaries; the Phoenix, Unicorn, Siren, Caladrius, and Salamander) • *Beowulf* (Beowulf and the Dragon) • The Old English *Phoenix* (elaborate Phoenix story, derived from Lactantius) • Bestiaries (expanded *Physiologus* with additional classical beasts; the Griffin, Crocotta, Manticore, Yale, Cinnamon Bird, Basilisk, and Amphisbaena) • Albertus Magnus, *On Animals* (comprehensive natural history) • Jacobus de Voragine, *The Golden Legend* (lives of St. George, St. Martha, and St. Margaret) • *The Romance of Alexander* (animal marvels of India) • *The Voyage of St. Brendan* (the Island Beast) • *The Arabian Nights* (the seven voyages of Sinbad the Sailor; the Roc, Karkadan, and Island

Beast) • *The Letter of Prester John* (fictitious letter accepted as true; beasts in the fabled kingdom of the Emperor of all the Indias) • Giraldus Cambrensis, *Topography of Ireland* (the first eye-witness account of the Barnacle Goose) • Marco Polo, *Travels* (the Roc of Madagascar and the Salamander) • Odoric of Pordenone, *The Journal of Friar Odoric* (the Vegetable Lamb of China) • Sir John Mandeville, *Travels* (fictitious work accepted as true; contains a famous passage about the Griffin)

Renaissance: Antonio Pigafetta, *Magellan's Voyage* (the Bird of Paradise) • Samuel Purchas, *Purchas His Pilgrimes* (first-person mariners' accounts of Mermaids) • Olaus Magnus, *History of the Goths, Swedes, and Vandals* (the first descriptions of the Sea Serpent and the Giant Squid or Kraken—sea monsters on Olaus's map of Scandinavia) • Ambroise Paré, *Of Monsters and Prodigies* (the Bishop Fish and Monk Fish) • John Gerard, *Herball* (eye-witness account of the Barnacle Goose) • Edward Topsell, *The Historie of Foure-Footed Beastes* (English version of Conrad Gesner's *Historia Animalium*; the Lamia, Leucrota, Manticore, and Catoblepas) • Sir Thomas Browne, *Vulgar Errors*, and Alexander Ross, *Arcana Microcosmi* (debate over the existence of beasts we now regard as mythical).

Secondary Sources

• Allen, Judy, and Jeanne Griffiths. *The Book of the Dragon*. London: Orbis, 1979.

• Borges, Jorge Luis. *The Book of Imaginary Beings*. 1957. Reprint. New York: Avon Books, 1970.

• Cooper, J.C. *Symbolic and Mythological Animals*. London: Harper Collins, 1992.

• Costello, Peter. *The Magic Zoo: The Natural History of Fabulous Animals*. New York: St. Martin's Press, 1979.

• Fox-Davies, A.C. *A Complete Guide to Heraldry*. London: Thomas Nelson and Sons, 1961.

• Gould, Charles. *Mythical Monsters*. 1886. Reprint. New York: Crescent Books, 1989.

• Graves, Robert. *The Greek Myths*. 1955, 1960. Reprint. Mt. Kisco, N.Y.: Moyer Bell Limited, 1988.

• Hargreaves, Joyce. *Hargreaves New Illustrated Bestiary*. Glastonbury, England: Gothic Image, 1990.

• *Larousse Encyclopedia of Mythology*. London: Paul Hamlyn, 1966.

• Leach, Maria, ed. *Funk and Wagnalls Standard Dictionary of Folklore, Mythology and Legend*. New York: Funk and Wagnalls Company, 1949.

• Ley, Willy. *Exotic Zoology*. New York: Viking, 1959.

• Nigg, Joseph. *The Book of Fabulous Beasts: A Treasury of Writings from Ancient Times to the Present*. New York: Oxford University Press, 1999.

• Payne, Ann. *Medieval Beasts*. London: The British Library, 1990.

• Shuker, Dr. Karl. *Dragons: A Natural History*. New York: Simon and Schuster, 1995.

• South, Malcolm, ed. *Mythical and Fabulous Creatures; A Sourcebook and Research Guide*. Westport, Conn.: Greenwood Press, 1987.

• White, T. H. *The Book of Beasts*. 1953. Reprint. New York: Dover, 1984.

Index

Credits

Quarto would like to acknowledge and thank the following illustrators:

Veronica Aldous: pages 23, 61, 66, 87, 117.
Greg Becker: pages 6-9, 27, 45, 56, 65, 72, 84, 94, 103, 108, 114.
Janie Coath: page 48.
Mark Duffin: pages 1-5, 14/15, 22, 31, 32, 36/37, 39, 44, 46/47, 51, 52, 67, 68, 70, 74/75, 76/77, 85, 86, 90, 92, 96, 99, 100, 104, 106/107, 109, 119, 120.
Griselda Holderness: pages 20, 41, 50, 55, 93.
Martin Jones: pages 16/17, 34, 42, 53, 59, 80, 88, 97, 105, 113, 121.
Olivia Rayner: pages 24, 33, 69, 83, 101, 118.
Rob Sheffield: pages 10-13, 18, 28, 38, 62, 98, 111.
Erica-Jane Waters: pages 30, 71, 79.

The author would like to dedicate this book to Esther and thank the following: editor Paula Regan and art editor Sally Bond; Oliver Monk, David Rea, Larry Dunning, Gary Reilly, and Marjorie Muzzillo for technical and editorial support; and Joey, Kelly, Jill, Jessie, Jayce, Max, and Cassidy for their delight in fantastic creatures.

Credits... Credits... Credits...